The Ladder to Success:

12 Leadership Steps for Children and Teens to

Accomplish a Rewarding Career and a Great Life

Noel D. Crum

Scenarios by Dr. Rocky Wallace

Copyright © 2018 by Noel D. Crum

Published by Ladder Publishing USA

All rights reserved. No portion of this book may be reproduced, stored in a retrieval system, or transmitted in any form or by any means – electronic, mechanical, photocopy, recording, scanning, or other – except for brief quotations in critical reviews or articles, without the prior written permission of the publisher.

ISBN 978-1-7324561-0-5

For more information about The Ladder to Success, including how to order more copies of the book or to contact the authors about speaking engagements, please visit the following website:
laddertosuccess.org

Contents Page

Forward

Acknowledgments

Introduction — Growing Leaders: What is Missing?

Step 1 - Developing Strengths and Talents

Step 2 - Motivation Understood

Step 3 - Failing Up the Ladder to Success

Step 4 - Responsibility Builds Self-Discipline and Self-Confidence

Step 5 - Attitude Will Determine Your Altitude

Step 6 - Cultivating Positive Communication Skills

Step 7 - Foster a Competitive Spirit

Step 8 - Two P's in a Pod — Perseverance and Perfection

Step 9 - Unlocking the Potential in a Difficult Child

Step 10 - Use Goal Setting and Visualization to Reach the Top

Step 11 - Discovering the Right Career Pathway to Future Success

Step 12 - Servant Leadership: The Final Step to Enjoying a Life of Success

Closing Thoughts and a Challenge for Action

References

Recommendations for Further Reading

About the Authors

Foreword

First, let me begin by introducing myself. My name is Noel Crum. I have spent the vast majority of my professional career as an educator and school administrator. My wonderful wife Stacy and I have been married for over twenty years, and we are the proud parents of three children – Reiley, Ally, and Sawyer, who have been growing up faster than I could write this book.

I would like to describe what this book is and is not. I am not a clinical psychologist, and this book is not an education based scientific study filled with laboratory or clinical experiments. I think the world already has enough of that approach.

When it comes to human interaction, I believe that observations and real-life experiences are the best ways to understand solutions to problems. Helping children become successful adults is far too complex of a topic with many different variables to even consider taking a scientific approach to understand it. Instead, this book is a common sense approach to understanding very important issues facing our youth today. I am not a scientist, and I do not claim to know everything. However, what I do know is that my experiences as an educator, administrator, and a parent have provided me with a unique perspective gained by examining the behavior and habits of thousands of children and their parents.

I have also studied leadership development for approximately 30 years, and my goal in this book is to take what I have learned from others along with my own observations and apply this knowledge to the topic of raising successful children. I have witnessed many students who utilized the characteristics outlined in this book to accomplish great things in their lives. I hope you find the practical ideas in this book to be insightful yet simple enough to quickly apply to your daily life.

This book is perfect for parents, guardians, grandparents, aunts, and uncles. However, this book is also vital for teachers, administrators, and coaches. Basically, anyone who has an impact on a child's life (from early childhood through college) would benefit from the insight provided here. Even teens, college students or young adults could read and directly gain a new perspective through these 12 steps on achieving lifelong success. I have thoroughly enjoyed writing this book, and I hope you find the end result helpful in guiding the young people in your life on the right path to becoming successful adults and our future leaders.

– Noel D. Crum

Acknowledgments

A very special thank you to John Robinson and Sloane Allyson Crum for illustrations and work designing the cover and to Caleigh Smith, Rachelle Burchett, Marsha Colvin, Bob Gound, Will Kaitain, and Adam Allison whose assistance with editing was a huge contribution to this work. Also, thank you to the Kentucky Valley Educational Cooperative and the leadership of Dr. Jeff Hawkins and Dr. Dessie Bowling who have been very supportive of this work. Finally, thank you to Bob Hutchison and Paul Castle who have provided support and advice that were critical to the completion of this book.

Dedication

This book is dedicated to the many educators, parents and other leaders who are down in the trenches modeling principled leadership for our young people every day. You are impacting the future more than you will ever know. Thank you.

On a personal note, I would like to dedicate this book to my grandparents along with my mother and aunt who always instilled me with so much love and encouragement and to my wife Stacy and my children Reiley, Ally, and Sawyer who support and inspire me every day to be a great leader.

– Noel Crum

Introduction — Growing Leaders: What is Missing?

The headline read, "Meth bust leads to two arrests."

A tip led police to a home where they discovered an active meth lab and a teen girl unresponsive. Paramedics revived the teen, and she was taken to an area hospital where she was treated for an apparent drug overdose.

Local police arrested 21-year old Roger Dawson for the manufacture of methamphetamines. Also, after being released from the hospital, the teen girl was arrested as an accomplice to the crime. Both Dawson and the unnamed teen are being held in the regional jail awaiting a court appearance on the charges.

Unfortunately, news stories like the one above are all too common today and are happening all across the world. While this story has been altered slightly to protect a couple of the individuals, it is based on true facts that impacted someone I know very well from my community.

The girl in this story, Cassandra, was addicted to meth and faced monumental odds of overcoming this horrible affliction. Her relationship with the young man who was arrested in this story nearly destroyed her life as he introduced her to a world of drug abuse. While the thought of being locked up behind bars is unimaginable for most people, it was the consequence that actually saved Cassandra's life. Fortunately, her time in prison allowed her to overcome her addiction and begin the arduous road to self-recovery. After her release from jail, she moved in with family members in another state. She beat monumental odds and made a full recovery. She now has a family and a stable life. However, the young man in this story did not have a positive outcome as destructive decisions eventually cost him his life.

The sad truth is we hear so many of these news stories today that we often become desensitized to the enormity of the issues facing our youth. Many people think these problems will never touch their families. I have heard people say, "If only they had raised their children right, this would not have happened." In reality, every young person is at risk of being sucked into the gravitational pull of a dark hole, so to speak. And when they do make poor choices, many never return from that dark place.

Our awareness of this terrible problem is very important, but it is only the first step in solving a crisis of this tragic magnitude. It is easy to point out things in society that need to be fixed, but it is a completely different matter to find meaningful solutions to perpetual problems. The keys to solving these enormous problems are the meat and potatoes of this book.

At this point, it is important for me to identify a common misconception that seems to be growing worse as our ever-changing world progresses. In today's society, we often put our emphasis on treating symptoms instead of identifying actual causes of our problems. Let me give you an analogy to help explain this point. If you had a persistent cough for a few days, you might go to a local department store and purchase some cough syrup. If you took that cough syrup for a week, and you still had the cough, you would probably go to a doctor who might give you some prescription strength cough syrup. If you took that medicine for a couple of weeks and you still had the persistent cough, have you been treating a symptom or a cause?

Obviously, something is causing you to have a persistent cough. Taking cough syrup only treats the symptom you are experiencing, but it does not treat what is causing you to have the persistent cough. More importantly, it logically does not define the reason why you are ill. You might have a sinus infection or some other illness that is making you continually cough, but until you find the actual source of your sickness, it will be difficult to permanently stop the coughing.

Now, let's take this same comparison and use it to address the problems we face today with drug abuse and underage drinking and tobacco use. Dating back to the 1980's with Nancy Reagan's slogan, "Just Say No to Drugs" or common slogans such as, "Don't Drink and Drive," many great agencies and individual celebrities have launched positive messages telling people not to do harmful or self-destructive things. However, all of these media campaigns are doing nothing more than treating symptoms rather than addressing the underlying cause of the problems. The focus is on how to tell people what not to do instead of sharing the feeling or emotions of the destructive behavior.

Don't get me wrong. I applaud the people who have given their time and resources to promote positive messages informing people of the dangers involved with this type of behavior, but the question is whether this approach is really tackling the problems that we face today. If you buy into the fact that we have a serious dilemma on our hands, then it is important that we find the actual causes of the problem rather than continuing to treat the symptoms. When exploring these issues, one question keeps coming to mind. "What could possibly cause so many young people to be led down the wrong path and begin participating in self-destructive behaviors? Fifty years ago, these problems did not seem to be so severe. What elements are missing from today's youth that could have led to this crisis?"

When I was growing up, I was often told the following statement, "If you encounter something that seems too good to be true, then it probably is too good to be true." In most cases, I agree with this premise. But when looking for the missing ingredient in today's youth, I think the solution is not complex or difficult to find. Instead, it is so simple that I can identify it in one word – LEADERSHIP.

Now, I know you may be asking how leadership can be the answer to so many serious issues facing our youth today. However, if you look closely at the problems we are currently experiencing, it is clear we have developed an entire generation of followers. When people are followers, peer pressure will often dictate their behavior. As a matter of fact, young leaders today are far and few between.

Many people might even wonder if there are any real young leaders out there anymore.

Unfortunately, there are a lot of people with leadership skills that many of us don't want to acknowledge today. Gang leaders and drug dealers definitely have leadership traits even though they use their skills of influence to create negative outcomes. Don't think for one second that these misguided people are not powerful leaders. When we have a generation of followers, it is naturally easy to see how young people can go down the wrong path following deceptive leaders with improper intentions.

Just think, Adolph Hitler had some of the most influential leadership skills in recorded history as evidenced by his guiding a nation into committing unspeakable acts of violence and bloodshed. Hitler had meticulously studied staff publications, essays on war tactics, understood military literature, and was one of the world's most influential orators. However, we don't often rank him among lists of great leaders. The difference is that he didn't use his leadership skills to better those around him.

Instead, if we can equip our young people with positive influential leadership skills, they can better make the right decisions for themselves. Then, when faced with peer pressure from the wrong people, they can march to the beat of their own drums and say no to the harmful and self-destructive temptations that plague our society.

To this point, we have only been discussing destructive decisions by youth, but many of you may be reading this book to look for solutions to specific issues with your own child or particular students you may work with as a teacher or coach. A child in your life may be suffering from ADHD or other learning disabilities or even something on the autism spectrum. Maybe a child in your life is performing poorly in school or is consistently facing an anger management problem or other behavior issues. If there is an obstacle in a child's life, the 12 steps outlined in this book can make a positive and lasting difference. Following these steps can help pull a child away from that dark void we discussed earlier and instead can potentially paint for them a much brighter future.

What if the significant child in your life is gifted or if you teach a whole group of gifted students? What if your child is an above average student who is just spinning his or her wheels? The truth is that many young people fall into positive friend groups and don't go down dangerous paths. The question for these young people is whether or not they are achieving their full potential and are headed for a life of success and happiness. Too many young adults are wandering through life with no direction or plan to achieve personal or career goals. Some might think this is just a generational curse, but a deeper examination reveals the actual root cause is once again a lack of leadership skills.

Regardless of socioeconomic status or education level, it is becoming clear to see that leadership is the missing ingredient in the lives of many young people today. In order to get a grip on how to fix this dilemma, let's first examine how these important principles have been collapsing for many decades. Here, we will focus on three primary reasons for the erosion of youth leadership values.

First and foremost, there is the old adage that says, "I don't want my children to face the same struggles I did growing up." So, instead of allowing our children to make mistakes and learn from them, most parents try to do more for their children and try to steer them away from the little realities in life that help shape our individual character and give us confidence to make decisions for ourselves. We don't want to see our children fail at anything, or experience the pain of losing, but in reality, most of us wouldn't be where we are today without our failures.

If Thomas Edison had been brought up in this type of environment, we may not have such modern conveniences as the light bulb or the motion picture camera. Edison believed that many people too often stopped trying when success was just around the corner.

Many children (and adults) today fit this description. Children are now accustomed to having things spoon-fed to them, and they often expect success to be waiting at the end of every activity. When encountered with failure, the first instinct is to get angry and quit. Thank goodness Edison learned from his mistakes and didn't give up on the journey to his many inventions. Edison embodied the perspective that obstacles are actually opportunities to be had and conquered. (We will further explore the importance of failure in raising successful children in Step 3 of this book.)

A second reason for the erosion of youth leadership values is the evolution of the Information Age. Through the explosion of technology and the Internet, children are exposed to so many things today that were not possible thirty years ago. Digital cable and satellite services have provided us with literally hundreds of viewing choices twenty-four hours a day, seven days a week, and 365 days a year. If children are not watching television, then they are certainly on the computer or in front of a video game system.

While the Internet definitely provides children with many great educational resources, there are also many options with inappropriate content such as chat rooms and websites containing graphic and sexual images. Please don't take this statement wrong. I am not an out of touch person who fails to see the importance of technology in today's society, but I am saying that children can quickly get lost in this sea of cyberspace which encourages a lot of mindless activity, not to mention exposure to a great deal of misinformation.

Many children have replaced creative playing, true social interaction, and involvement in extracurricular activities with time immersed in technology. Those "old fashioned" activities helped develop confidence and leadership skills. The end result of the many conveniences and advancements of the Information Age is many children who are desensitized to the importance of human interaction and who often lack individuality and social skills.

The third primary reason that youth leadership values are quickly vanishing is today's educational system. This is an area in which I have vast experience, and an area I see riddled with great misunderstanding from the general public. There is a common misconception in the world today that schools and teachers must push children harder and cover more material than in the past in order to keep up with our fast-paced society.

And there is a push, especially in the United States, to have all children master highly advanced levels of math and science along with other core areas. There is also a remarkable effort to hold schools and teachers accountable for rapid progress through numerous assessments.

With such a focus on data, schools are being unfairly forced into showing progress on annual exams that often compare different pools of students. For example, in the state of Kentucky, students used to be given a reading assessment in tenth grade and a mathematics assessment in eleventh grade to meet state and national requirements. To be deemed successful, each school had to show higher test scores from one year's tenth grade students in reading over the previous year's tenth grade students, even though the populations were not the same. This was also true for eleventh graders in math.

Now, I am not a mathematician, but I feel confident in saying there is little reliability in comparing two different student populations on an exam that expects each year's group to eclipse the previous one. This would be the same as asking a high school or college basketball coach to win more games and score more points each season of his coaching career. Even though he might graduate the majority of his starting lineup one year, he would be expected to have a better season the following year. I hope you can see the total lack of common sense behind the American government's push for excellence in education.

I know you may be asking what this has to do with the erosion of youth leadership values, but I can assure you it has a great deal to do with this dilemma. This international push for data driven assessments has been accompanied by requirements for more core classes, especially high-level math courses. Now, as an educator and a school administrator, I am completely in favor of offering students high-level academic course offerings. However, I am also in favor of meeting the needs of each child.

Unfortunately, the requirements that are being imposed on all students have created a cookie-cutter approach to education that has resulted in a great reduction of the programs offered today in our schools. Every year, more schools are cutting out programs such as music, art, and career and technical education. Physical education and good old-fashioned recess have also been reduced to a minimum in many schools, and with the new set of obstacles already being faced by our children in the Information Age, it is easy to see why poor leadership skills and even obesity are enormous problems today with our youth.

The reduction and elimination of academic and technical programs are only part of the problem. An equally serious issue is the narrowing of the curriculum in the core subject areas in our schools. A better way to phrase this is "teaching the test." Each year, as schools are forced to raise test scores, refinements are made in many schools to focus only on core areas of the content that have been identified by the governing education bodies to be eligible test items. As you can imagine, this often eliminates or greatly reduces the significance of elective subject areas that can greatly shape our students' lives.

I would like to take a moment here to make an important point. My statements are not a knock against teachers, administrators, or schools in general. As a matter of fact, I think teachers and administrators are doing a wonderful job today. Unfortunately, they are currently under such tremendous stress that many might consider a job as an air traffic controller to try to lighten their work load. Although this statement is a little sarcastic, I am sure that many school employees would agree with the analogy. For the most part, our schools are doing a great job of educating children, and I think all schools should have high standards. However, high stakes testing initiatives are rapidly disintegrating many of the qualities that made our schools successful in the 20th Century.

I feel this misconception concerning our educational system comes naturally to most people. Think about it. Everyone has been a student at one time, so most people easily feel very knowledgeable about the topic of education. On the other hand, using this logic would be similar to assuming a person would be able to make sound medical diagnoses because he or she once was a patient in a doctor's office. It also sounds very appealing when congressional leaders and legislators talk about setting high standards in education and the need to hold schools accountable.

I know I used to share the same beliefs before I entered the field of education. My experience as a teacher quickly exposed me to the vastly different needs of the students in my classroom. Today, it is evident to me that our schools are graduating many students who are severely lacking in leadership skills and are unprepared to succeed as an adult. If we would change the focus away from high stakes testing and place more emphasis on personalized learning and developing the talents and leadership skills of individual students, our schools could get back to the business of teaching students instead of a test.

Now that I have identified what I believe to be the three primary reasons for the erosion of youth leadership values today, we can begin the process of understanding the solutions for this enormous problem. I am sure many more reasons can be identified, but I think this is sufficient evidence to explain what has happened to the values and leadership structure that were in place a half-century ago.

Here, I want to focus on the keys for building successful youth leadership skills and in turn raising children who become successful and happy adults. Please keep in mind that I am not trying to reinvent the wheel here. The following steps to success are primarily built on principles that have been taught by some of the world's greatest leadership experts along with several new approaches I have developed. What I have tried to accomplish is to break down this vast amount of information and identify concepts that apply directly to the development of leadership in our youth.

After a great deal of real-life observations and examination of data, I have identified twelve steps that I will explain over the next several chapters. Most chapters will conclude with a scenario like the one below written by co-author Rocky Wallace. These scenarios are designed to illustrate the points outlined under each step. A set of questions will also be presented at the end of each chapter to encourage meaningful thinking and hopefully discussions among parents, grandparents, teachers, coaches and school administrators.

We all make an impact on the children in our lives. The steps in this book hold the keys to make that impact positive and to promote the leadership characteristics necessary for our children to achieve great success in all of life's endeavors. Now let's start the journey!

What Could Have Been"

John was raised in a principled home, with loving parents, grandparents, and other family role models who certainly gave him a head start on "making it" in this world. When he hit his teenage years, some friends were already dabbling in some bad habits that were destructive, and John himself began to question some of the core values he had been raised by.

Thankfully, he stayed focused on "doing the right thing", and his faith, and he went on to college. There, as many college students do, he went through a period of self-centeredness and self-importance that was disappointing to his parents and community back home. And, after a while, he even admitted to himself that he didn't like what he saw in the mirror anymore. He was confused, depressed, had low self-esteem, and finally dropped out of school when his girlfriend got pregnant and he was forced to get married at the age of twenty-one.

Later, as he began to realize what he had thrown away, John was bitter over the easier road he thought he had chosen. His job was boring, his wife was unhappy because he was unhappy, and his three kids seemed to be making the same mistakes he made—underachieving, not sure about what they really believed, experimenting with this and that. They seemed to be like leaves blowing in the wind—just as he recalled what his life was like as a child and teen.

John finally gave up one day, selling out for a new life with another woman, and simply told his wife as he walked out the door, "It could have been different, Honey. I could have been somebody. And you would have been happy, I would have been happy, our kids would have been raised in a happy home. But back there in college, when I had my whole life ahead of me, and the world seemed like such a carnival every day, I don't remember *anybody* taking me under their wing and coaching me about how to be a leader. And I don't remember anyone really doing it back in high school, or middle school, or elementary school either."

"Yes, we studied *books*, we took *tests*, and we worshipped our ball teams. But what about ol' John? Mom and Dad were so busy making ends meet, and my teachers were so busy keeping a school full of kids from getting into mischief, as I look back now, did anyone really show me how to build a smart plan for my life?...No. Not one."

"So, I'm outta here. I'm a failure as a man, I'm a failure as a husband, I'm a failure as a father, I'm a failure as a son…Go figure. 'Cause way back there when I was still a kid, I had a whole lot goin' for me. But now at the ripe age of thirty-five, I'm just a shell of the man I used to be. My boss even told me on my evaluation last week that it was time I started being a leader! OK, sounds like a good idea after all these years. But, tell me this–how?"

Questions for Reflection

1. What is your school's philosophy regarding total menu of student services? Are co-curricular, extra-curricular, clubs, and other 'life skill' activities increasing, or on the decrease?

2. How is technology shaping the lives of the children in your life? Do they keep a healthy balance between working on the Internet, and getting involved in other more "off line", hands-on activities?

3. What is your school doing to promote inquiry and inventive learning? Is creative exploration and new learning a focus? What is your school doing to teach students to be leaders?

4. Do you feel the current assessment focus across the state and nation is increasing the quality of instruction, or is it to a boiling point and now hindering the type of learning for our children to succeed in today's world?

5. Are the children in your life receiving any instruction about leadership either at home or at school? If so, how early does it begin?

John C. Maxwell (2007), in Talent Is Never Enough, *cautions that there is more to living an effective life than having potential. One has to know how to apply the core principles of integrity-driven leadership if expecting to rise above the mediocrity of the status quo.*

Developing Strengths and Talents
Step 1

The first and perhaps the most important key to rearing successful children and teens who develop positive leadership skills is recognizing and improving strengths and talents. If a person can understand his or her areas of strength at an early age, it will be much easier to develop a high level of self-confidence. This leads to higher levels of success and greater leadership skills. Unfortunately, this idea goes against the grain of the society we live in today. We currently face a time when being at least average at everything is the focus of our daily lives. Instead of identifying strengths and talents, schools and many parents are more worried about identifying weaknesses and concentrating time on improving those weaknesses.

I was guilty of committing these mistakes personally, and if you think about it, most everybody today seems to do the same thing. If we have an area of weakness, we focus time trying to improve that area of weakness. I continued to believe this fallacy until several years ago when I had the opportunity to hear leadership expert Dr. John Maxwell explain his approach to developing strengths. At one of his lectures I attended in Ashland, Kentucky in 2003, he made the statement that if a student comes home with a report card, and he or she has an "A" in English and a "C" in math, most parents would typically make their child work harder in math and just be happy to maintain the good grade in English.

Instead, Maxwell indicated that parents should realize that their child's area of strength is English, and the child should focus even harder on that subject. Now, this concept goes against much of what we are used to practicing in education. However, Maxwell puts this into perspective through a scale of 1-to-10, on which he suggests we rank our different skill levels. He contests that even with great practice and hard work; a person can only improve two or three numbers on the scale. For example, let's say that Jane wants to be an artist, but her current skill level in the area of art is a two on a scale of 1-to-10. Even with lessons from the finest art teachers in the world, her skill level in the area of art would probably only improve to a four or five on a scale of 1-to-10. If the lessons and practice take her from terrible to average in the area of art, consumers still won't buy her paintings and she will be left wondering why she spent so much time in an area that did not give her successful results. On the other hand, if her skill level in art is a seven on a scale of 1-to-10, and she works really hard to improve her skill level up to a nine or ten, people will be lining up to buy her paintings. I will also give you a real-life personal application of this philosophy. I have always considered myself to be a good problem-solver and idea generator. I seem to have a knack for coming up with strategies to improve a situation. However, after I have laid out the plan for fixing a problem, I have always faced many struggles with completing organizational details. This problem has always perplexed me and has at times reduced my self-confidence.

I have often started projects and failed to complete them because I was so slow at carrying out the necessary details. I have repeatedly tried to improve this weakness of mine, but I have never seemed to achieve a high level of success in this area. Instead, I found that I was devoting so much time to this deficiency that I was spending less time in my areas of strength and thus reducing my overall performance level in my job.

As soon as I was able to understand that I was wasting precious time trying to improve a weakness instead of devoting time to improve my areas of strength, I was able to let go of several years of frustration and disappointment. Through this realization, I was able to look to others I work with to help out more in my areas of weakness, and I have been able to spend more time working in the areas where I can make a real positive difference. It is a very liberating experience to discover your weaknesses and admit them to your friends, family, and co-workers. By doing this, you create a stronger sense of teamwork and closer relationships with those around you.

The application to take from my personal example in terms of raising successful children is that the earlier you can identify a child's strengths and spend time trying to maximize those areas, the greater opportunity the child has to become successful as an adult.

Once those strengths are identified, there is one other key ingredient that is necessary for children and adults to achieve success in their areas of talent. That ingredient is passion. This has led me to develop a basic formula that can help young people and even adults excel in life: Passion + Talent = Success. I like to think of this model as similar to a chemical reaction. When we find those instances in life where passion and talent collide, the result is success. This also reminds me of an early 1980's television commercial for Reece's Peanut Butter Cups. When a person eating a chocolate bar bumps into a person eating peanut butter, and when the chocolate falls into the peanut butter, they both discover a delicious taste.

> *"... a basic formula that can help young people and even adults excel in life: Passion + Talent = Success."*

The collision of talent and passion is similar because alone, each is a good trait to have, but when combined together, something really special occurs. This is an important formula for parents and other adults to remember when working with children because one often exists without the other. Some children might be very gifted in an area but might not enjoy the activity at all.

For instance, my youngest son Sawyer was good at hitting a baseball when he was very young, and I strongly encouraged him to play. I even helped coach his team, but it was apparent that he did not have a passion for the game like I did. I wanted him to share my passion, but it clearly was not there. However, he was also talented at kicking a soccer ball, and he had a tremendous passion for the sport. Even though I loved baseball and knew relatively little about soccer, I did not sign him up for baseball the following season, and instead, he began playing soccer–which he still actively participates in today.

This experience reminded me of a friend I had in high school whose father pressured him to play football even though he was not really passionate about it. He was very talented at football, but his resentment for the sport grew, and he never played again after graduating from high school. Unfortunately, many parents try to live out their unrealized dreams through their children. Many parents' lack of contentment in their own lives will flow over into their parenting which leads to negative outcomes for their children.

It is also important to note that unlike talent, passion can vary greatly over time, especially in younger children. A child can seem passionate about an activity for a month and then act like it is the worst thing in the world the next month. Just because children show an immediate passion for an activity, we should not drown them in the activity. We need to encourage participation in a variety of activities so we can take time to evaluate the child's level of passion and talent over an extended period of time. If that passion remains constant and the child shows signs of giftedness, we need to devote time to help cultivate and grow that talent.

Also, we should not completely dismiss an area of talent if the child does not show any passion for the activity. We should not pressure the child just because he or she is talented in an area, but we may want to reintroduce the activity at various points in the future because passion for an activity can develop with maturity.

On the other side of the coin, many children are passionate about an activity, but they have little talent or ability in that area. For example, some children may love to sing, but they have no natural ability. Without any singing talent, the opportunity to achieve success is slim. This reality can be very difficult for parents when a child enjoys an activity but has little or no talent in that area. If the child is having fun participating in the activity, we should continue encouraging involvement, but it would not be prudent to devote excessive time in just that area. That activity may become a hobby for the child to enjoy, but we should definitely keep searching for areas of giftedness.

I can give you a good personal example of continuing to participate in an activity where I have a low level of skill. I thoroughly enjoy playing golf, but I have very little talent in that area. However, I look forward to playing every chance I get. The difference for me is that I don't make it the focus of my life. I tell others when I play that I am not talented at golf, but I love playing. This actually allows me to enjoy the sport even more because I don't get mad at myself when I hit a bad shot. I recognize my limitations, and this allows me to set my own personal goals rather than comparing myself to others who are gifted in the area of golf.

I also want to take time to note that I don't endorse the idea of totally forgetting about a given area of weakness. If the area of weakness is something that is required or is a necessary component of our daily lives, it will be important to at least devote enough time to reach an acceptable level of proficiency. For instance, if writing is an area of weakness for you, it is not practical to completely avoid practicing in the area of writing. While you will probably never be a published author, it is important to learn necessary writing skills to communicate effectively in life, including writing a resume and letter of application.

One other essential note is that if reading is an area of weakness, it is very important to work on this deficiency. While one may never be an outstanding reader, it is vital to have good reading skills in order to succeed in any discipline in life.

As a parent, teacher, or significant adult in the life of a child, it is critical to help children gain an understanding of their talents, and work diligently to focus on improving skills in their identified areas of strength. Just think, if your child or student becomes a 9 or a 10 in his or her strength zone and has a high level of passion, great success will soon follow! This can be one of the most important steps that adults can take to help young people achieve success.

"But Daddy, I Love Horses"

Bobby Sue dreaded to come home from school. She knew her parents would ask her as soon as she walked through the door what she made on her report card.

"Bobby Sue! What's this C in English, and C in math? I told you last semester that if you didn't get these two subjects up, things might have to change around here!" Her Dad was obviously frustrated, and let the screen door slam on his way to the barn to feed.

"Mom, what about my A's in science, and social studies, and art, PE, and music?"

"Little girl, your father is still kicking himself 'cause he never went to college like he should've. He had a scholarship to a little school a few hours away. Was a free ride. But, he just had to take the first job that came along 'cause he thought he needed to make good money right out of high school."

"I've always wondered why he seemed so discontent, Mother. Dad just seems to always be restless. What do you think he would have studied in college?"

"He's told me that he had his heart set on history. As you know, he absolutely loves anything that has to do with history. That's why we always take our family vacations to historic sites…I think he'd have been a teacher, Bobby Sue. Do you know, every time your father and I are over at your school, he gets this wistful look in his eye. I've watched him walk down the hall and just look in each room ever so intently, as if he's saying, "That's what I would have been great at. That's my passion."

"But Mom, it's not too late. If Dad loves history that much, and he'd love to teach it, why doesn't he enroll in classes down at the local community college, and chase his dream? You're always reminding us kids to dream big, and shoot for the stars."

"Because Bobby Sue, your dad has bills to pay, and a family to raise, and mainly, he has a whole lot of pride that he'd have to swallow if he went back to school at this age."

"Just seems such a shame Mom, that's all I'm saying."

Bobby Sue stopped abruptly, as her father came back from the barn.

"Bobby Sue, I know how much you love that horse of yours. And I know that you're one of the best riders in the 4-H show every summer. And I also know that you'd love to keep learning more and more about horses, and, what do they call it, equestrian studies? In fact, that bothers me. It seems it's all you really work hard at sometimes. So, tell you what we're going to do. Until you bring that English grade up to a A, and that math grade up to an A, I'm banning you from riding your horse. You'll have six weeks to re-focus your energy. And, if that doesn't help, maybe we need to sell your horse come summer."

Bobby Sue ran upstairs to her room, and threw herself on the bed—crying herself to sleep. And when she woke up the next morning, she put her book about equestrian science and vet school in the closet.

"How could I have ever thought I'd get to be a veterinarian some day?" She scolded herself as she looked in the mirror and got ready for school.

"I just don't have time for it...I don't have what it takes."

And now, years later, every great once in a while, when she's visiting her folks and down at her Dad's barn, Bobby Sue gets butterflies in her stomach as she smells the stall where she used to keep her horse. And she wonders what might have been—what could have been...Oh how she loves horses! Oh how she misses them so.

Questions for Reflection

1. Have you identified gifts in your children? If so, what are those areas of strength?

2. Are you providing opportunities for your children to discover their talents or passions?

3. What is a passion you have that you have put on the backburner?

4. Do your children or other young people you influence or mentor have a grasp on the importance of developing their 'strength zones'?

5. What are your memories of 'making good grades' when you were in school? Did some classes sometimes keep you from pursuing other courses where you had a stronger interest or more aptitude?

6. Are you a conformist, or non-conformist? How did the structure and routine of school help or hinder you in going deeper in the study of your favorite subjects?

7. Are you a lifelong learner? Do you have joy and fulfillment in most of your life's endeavors?

Marcus Buckingham and Donald O. Clifton (2001), in Now, Discover Your Strengths, *emphasize the wisdom of focusing on identified gifts and abilities, thus unleashing potential where there will be the greatest return.*

Motivation Understood
Step 2

Another key to developing successful youth leadership skills is somewhat more of an abstract, yet simple concept. A critical factor in raising successful children is centered on understanding motivation and how it impacts our decision-making process and our behavior. There are many different theories explaining the concept of motivation, but my experiences over the past two decades in education have helped me develop a simplistic approach to understanding how people are motivated. It is my belief that as humans, we are motivated in one of only two ways to do everything. We are either motivated intrinsically or by fear of consequences.

Let me take a moment to explain each type of motivation. I will first describe fear-based motivation which is actually very common in our daily lives. Ask yourself a simple question the next time you are in a hurry and are driving somewhere. How fast would you drive if you knew there were absolutely no police officers on the road and hence no chance of getting a speeding ticket? I know I would feel comfortable driving several miles over the speed limit if I knew I had no chance of receiving a ticket.

However, we know that the possibility of a police officer being just around the next curve always exists, and therefore, we usually stay within a close range of the speed limit. Our fear of the possible consequence of being pulled over by a police officer and receiving a ticket motivates us to obey the speed limit to at least a certain degree.

While that example is quite simple, think of all the things in your life that you avoid doing because of the fear of certain consequences. These fears may be based on possible embarrassment, rejection, or failure. Even the fear of unknown results may motivate you to not proceed with an idea or initiative. While most of us think of motivation as a positive thing that encourages us to do something, I hope you can see that we are just as often motivated to not do something.

This type of fear-based motivation is actually the basis of old school business principles that were prevalent in the 20th Century, and unfortunately many managers still employ this technique today. While this model is not called fear-based management, it is still based on the principles of motivation by fear. It is more commonly called an autocratic or top-down management style. Employees perform tasks they are told to complete by their bosses. The fear of being reprimanded or not earning a paycheck makes the employees complete their job tasks.

Unfortunately, when people are motivated by fear, creativity is often stifled, and many employees only give a strong effort when the boss is watching. Workers motivated by fear rarely stay late after work or do any of the little things that turn good efforts into great ones.

The other type of motivation is intrinsic. Merriam Webster's dictionary defines intrinsic as "belonging to the essential nature of a thing or occurring as a natural part of something." This type of motivation is one that is completely internal, and can appear to us in many different forms.

Intrinsic motivation can be an impulse to buy something or do something enjoyable. It can often be an indulgence such as a piece of cake for dessert. Or, it can be a positive action, such as helping out a friend or donating to a good cause. Intrinsic motivation can be a competitive drive to participate in a sport or play a board game. It might even be something as large as deciding to earn a college degree or applying for a new job. In each case, the decision to act is completely internal and not guided by fear. It is basically just doing something because you wanted to do it, not because you were afraid of what would happen if you didn't do it.

The decisions you make over the course of a day vary from extremely simple to complex, but all of them will hinge on fear or intrinsic motivation. Let's go through some examples of decisions you might make in a day. When you get up in the morning, you will probably take a shower and brush your teeth. You may not want to brush your teeth but the fear of having bad breath or getting cavities motivates you to brush them anyway. You may take a shower because it refreshes you and makes you feel good. If you don't like to take a shower, the fear of having body odor might motivate you to take one.

When you make your decision about breakfast, you might be motivated by fear to eat a bowl of bran cereal because you don't want to become unhealthy, or you might not eat at all because you are afraid of gaining weight. However, you might be motivated intrinsically to eat bacon, eggs, and pancakes because this food tastes good and you are craving it for breakfast.

After eating, you might go to work because you love your job and you enjoy going there every day. Or, you might hate your job, but you go because of your fear of being unemployed or having to look for a new job. If you are a college student, you might go to classes because you enjoy them and you want to learn something new, or you might be afraid of what your grade will be if you skip school.

Your decisions about lunch and dinner will also be guided by intrinsic motivation or by fear, just like breakfast. In your spare time that evening, you might be motivated intrinsically to watch a movie or go bowling, or even just spend quality time with family and friends. You might be motivated by fear to go work out for an hour at a local gym because you don't want to be out of shape. I hope you can see what a huge role that fear and intrinsic motivation play in our daily lives. As a matter of fact, I would argue that the only actions we perform in a day that are not governed by these two types of motivation are necessary body functions such as breathing and sleeping.

Now, you may be wondering how understanding the two types

of motivation is related to helping children develop positive leadership skills, but actually there is a strong connection. Through my experience as a school administrator, I have had the opportunity to observe many children and young adults make great decisions and become outstanding leaders. However, I have also had the unfortunate perspective of seeing students make destructive decisions and go down the wrong path. Earlier in the introduction of this book, I explained that developing positive leadership skills is the primary determinant of whether a young person will achieve success in life. I also explained how young followers can be steered in the wrong direction by leaders with bad intentions. Finally, I also explained the importance of discovering root causes of issues and not just treating symptoms.

With that understanding in mind, we can now dig deeper into the raw emotions and learned behaviors that determine whether someone will become a leader or a follower. While there are several other factors that we will discuss later in this book, motivation is the root that will determine whether a young person will blossom into a bright and wonderful leader or grow thorns and become a vine that follows the first path it finds.

Young people who are guided by intrinsic motivation tend to be more confident and are willing to take the necessary risks that leaders navigate to achieve success. On the other hand, young people who are controlled by fear will be afraid to stand up to peer pressure and will be easily led astray by negative leaders. The other alternative for those guided by fear is that they will become apathetic and stop taking part in new activities. The end result of this behavior is often an adult who lives a very mundane life, never looking for new opportunities to achieve success!

When examining people who have used intrinsic motivation to achieve success, there is one strong example that comes to my mind. I had the pleasure of teaching a student named Aaron Davis at Johnson Central High School, who has grown up to accomplish amazing things with his life. As a computer instructor during my first year of teaching back in 1996, I had the responsibility of teaching keyboarding skills to freshmen students. One of my class activities on the first days of school was to measure how fast my students could type as they entered the course. This would provide a good reference for me as a pre-test and later as a post-test to determine how much my students learned. I used an automated program called Touch Typing for Beginners.

Out of more than one hundred students that I had on my class rosters, Aaron was at the bottom of the list with only twelve words per minute. At the time, I thought this was kind of unusual, because he was in a selective track called the Commonwealth Diploma program, reserved for the top academic students. Also, he was very athletic and had excellent hand-eye coordination. One of his friends in the same class was typing thirty-five words per minute, and I could tell that it really bothered him that he was so unskilled in this area. Over the coming weeks, I noticed that any spare moment he had in class was spent completing drills on various lessons in the software program. As the year progressed, he and the other students in that Commonwealth class became so competitive that I began keeping a leader chart for each lesson to see who would hold the speed record.

Amazingly enough, by the end of that class, Aaron held some of the places on my class leaderboard as he could type over 100 words per minute on many of the lessons. However, he didn't stop there. Over his next three years of high school, he would stop by my room during breaks and complete lessons to try to break records on my leaderboard even though he was no longer in my class or getting a grade for it!

That high level of motivation combined with a strong competitive desire (which is a topic I will discuss in Step 7) should have clued me into the fact that Aaron would become extremely successful in his life. However, I could have never imagined the path that he would take to achieve great success and happiness.

After high school, Aaron chose to pursue a career as an engineer. He completed his civil engineering degree at the University of Kentucky, and he began a successful career with a mining company. Aaron also got married to a young lady who was beginning her law degree, and he started a family of his own. After starting his career, Aaron became active in a local church. When his minister became ill, the church leaders asked Aaron if he would assist with the preaching duties. Aaron jokes that his first sermon rated as high in quality as twelve words per minute rated in his computer keyboarding class; however, Aaron again found the intrinsic motivation to accept the challenge. He began studying the Bible intensely and was soon holding local revival meetings and serving as associate minister in two area churches in addition to working full-time as an engineer.

Aaron had what most people would deem a wonderful life. However, he knew something was missing. While he had a very good job at that time, he had strong intrinsic motivation to change his career path. He decided to quit his job and enroll in law school. Now, how many people with a secure job and a family would take the risk of leaving their job to go back to school? The fear of leaving that security and having such little money for one's family would lead most people to stay in a job they didn't enjoy just because the compensation was good.

However, Aaron's intrinsic motivation guided him to pursue his dream. Today, he and his wife have started their own law firm, and he has developed into a highly successful minister. Aaron has completely memorized eighteen books in the New Testament and has preached sermons in ten different states. There is one thing for certain, Aaron has made decisions in his life based on intrinsic motivation, not on fear, and this is a primary factor in helping him enjoy a happy and successful life with his family today.

Hopefully as a significant person in the life of a child, you will work to encourage the young people in your world to understand the negative effects of fear. Also, by empowering children with the strength of understanding intrinsic motivation, they can couple that knowledge with the upcoming steps in the following chapters to achieve a complete and fulfilling life of happiness and success.

"Caleb's War"

"Come on honey, we're going to be late for the talent show at school." Caleb's mom rushed out the door with her purse and keys in one hand, and his baby sister hanging on her other shoulder. He moaned, and tried to gag so he might appear to throw up.

"Caleb, son, what on earth is bothering you? Let's go. You're on the schedule early tonight. Dad is meeting us from work, and I don't want you to miss your performance."

"But I don't want to play the piano in front of all of those people, Mom! I'm in the sixth grade now–I'm too old for this. Please, don't make me go." Caleb began to cry, and his mom did indeed wish that she could stay home too. These episodes were getting old, and she was beginning to wonder if maybe she was pushing her son too hard. After all, he was only twelve years old, and he had dreaded playing the piano in front of people from his very first recital.

But, she and his father had always taught Caleb to complete what he started, and to not let others down when he was needed. To cop out at this late stage would definitely leave the wrong impression with his principal, who had worked hard to put the talent show together.

"Caleb, tell you what I'll do. After tonight, we'll talk about you perhaps taking a break from piano lessons this summer. But, let's get going so we're not late. You owe it to your classmates and your school to do what you said you would do."

"I never said I would play the piano in the talent show this year, Mom. You e-mailed the principal and signed me up, remember?"

"And I'm never going to do that again, Caleb. We've invested quite a bit of money in your music lessons, but you know what? I'm tired too. It's not worth this tug of war every time you have to step up to the plate and show what you can do...Come on, let's go — we'll barely make it if we leave right now."

Caleb's stomach ached, and his hands were wet with sweat as he waited his turn to go up on stage and play his song. He was fifth in the order of performers, but it felt like two hours. Oh how he'd love to be home right now, out in the back yard, playing with his dog and having a relaxing evening — without pressure!

When his name was finally called, Caleb said a silent prayer and promised himself, "Remember, this is the last time. Mom promised. Go do your best."

As he struggled to get his hands to stop shaking, so he could at least get through the song, Caleb's dad stood in the back with tears in his eyes, and thought to himself, "What have we done to make him so nervous like this? That's not the same little boy who begged me to play ball, and to take piano lessons, and to learn to swim, and to build him a tree house — all in the same summer back when he had just finished first grade."

Perhaps because it was probably his last recital, ever, Caleb rose to the occasion, got focused, and played his song better than he had even practiced it at home. In fact, he nailed it! As he finished, and stood to give a polite bow, the crowd in the school gym raised up in unison and gave him a standing ovation—many of them remembering how he had struggled during the show in the past.

On the way home, Caleb's mom beamed with joy that only a mother can feel. "Now see there, what have I been telling you, Sweetie? You were awesome tonight. I was so proud of you!"

Caleb felt so good inside. He couldn't believe the adrenalin rush, and the internal satisfaction. And so, he changed his mind. He kept taking lessons. And he kept practicing. And he soon looked forward to his piano time with his teacher, Mrs. Vanwinkle. There was something about the challenge. He knew he could quit and never sit down to a piano again. But he had changed. He realized this was so good for him, and he loved the music, loved the self-discipline, even loved the pressure of learning a new, difficult song and eventually playing it for other people.

Ten years later, Caleb was giving the student address at his college graduation. His peers from the senior class had selected him to represent them on stage, and he was glad to do it. For, you see, Caleb had not forgotten how he let fear almost rob him of his love for playing music when he was back there in elementary school.

And he had not forgotten Mrs. Vanwinkle. In fact, he had invited her to be one of his guests on this very special day. And when he got up to give his talk, his knees didn't shake, his stomach didn't hurt, and his voice didn't quiver. He knew what he had to do. Something inside had been telling him for a long time that this day would come. He had actually looked forward to it. He had played in his mind over and over what it would be like, looking over the crowd and having the courage down deep inside to just go out there and hit a home run.

And he did. And his mom and dad cried, and the crowd stood and roared, and Caleb understood what it means to be motivated on the inside. It makes all the difference.

Questions for Reflection

1. Can you remember a time in your life when fear paralyzed your ability to perform a task? How did you feel?
2. Can you identify areas where fear is guiding the behavior of your children or students?
3. What current activities in your children's do they intrinsically enjoy?
4. Does your school or community concentrate on providing opportunities for children and youth that develop intrinsic life skills?
5. Have you ever, through internal determination, overcome a fear, or performed a difficult task that you didn't think you could do?
6. If we as adults often shy away from opportunities because of fear, what does this teach us in how we can better help young people to learn to intrinsically embrace new experiences?

Daniel Pink (2009), in Drive, presents a fascinating look at what motivates each of us as individuals. Much more than external forces, he reveals that the intrinsic drive inside every person is the real key.

Failing Up the Ladder to Success
Step 3

Let's start this chapter with a relatively simple question.

What is the opposite of success?

Failure?

That seems to be the overwhelming response to this question. Was that your first reaction? Although failure appears on the surface to be the opposite of success, that response is absolutely wrong! Let's dive a little deeper into this topic to find the true answer, and we can start by examining the following quote.

"I've missed more than 9,000 shots in my career. I've lost almost 300 games. Twenty-six times, I've been trusted to take the game-winning shot and missed. I've failed over and over and over in my career, and that is why I succeed."

Those words were spoken by Michael Jordan in a famous Nike commercial which illustrates how failure played a significant role in helping him achieve enormous success in his career. Most people would never look at Jordan's career in such a perspective, but this principle is at the heart of The Ladder to Success.

The topic of this chapter is a very perplexing subject for many parents and educators. Failure has such a negative connotation in today's society that we often will do anything to avoid it. Many people choose not to engage in any activity that might result in failure. However, some of the most successful people in history have used failure to initiate and obtain success.

It is my contention that there is an extremely fine line between success and failure. Many people believe that success and failure are at different ends of the spectrum and are polar opposites. Instead, it is my observation that success and failure are not opposites at all. Instead, I contend that not participating and quitting are the true opposites of both success and failure. I call this progression to achievement the Ladder to Success. To help you visualize this point, think of a ladder with four rungs. The rung at the bottom of the ladder is not participating or inaction and the next rung is quitting or withdrawal. The third rung is failure while the fourth and highest rung is success (see figure below).

When faced with an opportunity, choosing inaction means you are not going to climb up the ladder. Neither success nor failure is an option when you choose not to act at all. This is the fate of many people because they are so afraid of failing. There is an old adage on the basketball court which says you will miss 100 percent of the shots you do not take. While that statement seems obvious, it has great meaning when looking at the topic of success versus failure. Many players on the court will repeatedly choose to not shoot the basketball, even when they are wide open, because they are afraid of failure. However, these players never stop to think about having a zero percent chance for success when they choose not to take the open shot.

Quitting or withdrawal is one step higher on the ladder because action was initiated but then stopped. Often withdrawal is also the result of seeing failure as a possible result once an action has been initiated. Another possible cause for quitting is a lack of work ethic. Since we live in a society where we expect immediate gratification, a lot of people, especially many children and teens, tend to give up on activities if they feel it will require too much work or will take a long time before they achieve success.

In this model, failure is next on the ladder and is only one step away from success. This concept is hard for many to accept, but it makes sense if you think of it in terms of a couple of real-life instances. Sports provide some of the greatest examples of the fine line between success and failure. How many last second shots in a basketball game have missed by the narrowest of margins? Another centimeter in one direction or the other, and that loss could have been turned into an enormous victory. In events such as track and field, auto racing and horse racing, a fraction of a second often separates winning and losing.

As I discussed in the introduction, Thomas Edison was a perfect example of how failure is only one step away from success. When he was attempting to invent the light bulb, Edison experienced many failures. A journalist asked him if he felt like a failure and if he thought he should just give up. Edison is reported to have replied, "Young man, why would I feel like a failure? And why would I ever give up? I now know definitively over 9,000 ways that an electric light bulb will not work. Success is almost in my grasp." Eventually, after over 10,000 attempts, Edison climbed one more rung up the ladder and reached success by inventing the light bulb.

Success is the final rung on the ladder and is the culmination of overcoming thoughts of not participating and quitting along with battling through and learning from failures. Climbing through these obstacles is a natural part of the journey toward success, and it is not always a simple process as evidenced in Edison's long progression to inventing the light bulb. Sometimes we get stuck on the failure rung of the ladder, but just knowing that you are only one step from achieving a goal can help us stay focused on attaining ultimate success.

I know this is a difficult philosophy for many parents to digest as there is almost nothing worse than watching a child fail at something. However, robbing our youth of these life experiences erodes the confidence that is gained by learning from mistakes and turning those failures into successes. If children don't get the opportunity to actually feel these experiences, they may not be equipped to make the right decisions when parents are not there to steer them in the right direction. They will also lack the confidence to stand up to peer pressure and will likely become followers instead of leaders.

I am a great example of how fear of failure can prevent success. When I was in high school, I had several friends and was fairly popular, but I only went out on a couple of dates in my four years of school. There were plenty of girls who I found attractive, but like many other teenagers, I was so afraid of failure and rejection that I never asked any of them out on a date. Instead, I played it safe and chose to be friends each time I had an opportunity to approach a girl for a date. I carried this same fear of failure into other parts of my life. When faced with opportunities to run for student council at my school, I chose not to participate because I thought I may lose. Looking back at my high school years, I realize that my fear of failure in numerous areas prevented me from any possibility of achieving success.

On the other end of the spectrum, I had a friend who was completely the opposite of me in this perspective. This friend always dated some of the most attractive and popular girls in our school, and he always carried himself with a quiet confidence. I became very good friends with him later in high school and on into college. The better I got to know him, the more it became clear to me that the primary reason he was so successful was the fact that he had no fear of failure or rejection.

I actually learned that there were instances in his life where he had been rejected when asking a girl out on a date, but it really did not bother him. He even pointed out to me that if someone said no, what did you actually lose? It is not like you already had a relationship with that person and lost it. You did not have a relationship when you approached her for a date, and when she turned you down, you still did not have a relationship. What a great way to look at things! Unfortunately, the majority of young people and even adults choose to let fear of failure guide their decisions. After closer observations, I can see that many successful people I have encountered in my life achieved success in many different ways by not having a fear of failure.

My personal story is only one example of how the fear of failure prevents many of us from reaching success, and I am sure that some of you might be saying that you are not reading this to help teens get a date. That is definitely not the main point of this book, but it is a very important example of how we too often do not view failure as being one step away from success. By not advancing up the ladder at all, we tend to believe we are not failing. I contend that when faced with a good opportunity, choosing not to participate is the worst possible outcome because you are providing yourself with absolutely zero chance for success!

"... choosing not to participate is the worst possible outcome because you are providing yourself with absolutely zero chance for success!"

The dating example is only one of many situations where young people let their fear of failure get the best of them. How many students do not join athletic teams or participate in events that might put them on a stage in front of others? It would be hard to get a true percentage because many of these young people have suppressed their desires and interests so much that parents, teachers, and other adults are not even aware that an interest in something even exists.

Now, the big question is how to tackle this problem. Here is something to consider. Just think how little children between the ages of two and four love to be the center of attention. Many of them enjoy putting on a show in front of groups of family members, or sometimes in public areas. Often these children are put on a stage in prince and princess pageants or other local festival events. Years later, many of these same children could not be forced to perform in front of others, and they often say they cannot believe that they ever had the nerve to get on a stage when they were little.

Unfortunately for me, this is a clear case where my own

parenting has led me to see the importance of this example. My daughter was involved in pageants from before she could walk until a few years ago. She then decided that she wanted to start performing in the local theatre. She has also been consistently involved in singing, dance teams, and she even won a karaoke contest sponsored by our local radio station. The point is that she has never gone a long period of time without being on stage performing in front of others.

And furthermore, she has absolutely no hesitation about getting in front of people. She has experienced many successes and many failures. She won the overall talent competition in the Little Miss Kentucky pageant, but she has also walked away with nothing in many small pageants and talent competitions. However, she has developed a positive attitude about these experiences. She has little fear of failure, and she realizes that she has absolutely no chance for success if she does not participate. As a parent, I always strived to never react negatively about failures she experienced. Instead, I always tried to focus on what she could learn from the situation to achieve success the next time.

On the other hand, my oldest son is a completely different example. He was in a couple of "Little Prince Pageants" when he was young, and he had no fear of being in front of people by himself. However, after a long absence from being in front of others, my wife approached him about being in a local play, and he wanted no part of it at the time. I have noticed that he steers away from being alone in front of large groups.

Fortunately, he consistently played basketball or soccer throughout his childhood, and he does not have any anxiety about playing these sports in front of a group of people. However, in this setting, he is part of a group, and he has developed a comfort level because of his experiences. Only now do I realize that it would have been beneficial to have consistently provided him with experiences performing in front of others.

Now, I am not suggesting that parents throw their children out to the wolves. It is a totally different problem when parents are not there at all for their children. This is also true for teachers and coaches. It is essential for significant adults to be there for children to provide encouragement and moral support.

But when a child does fail at an activity, we must also be there to show how close they are to achieving success. We must teach them that they have almost made it to the top of the ladder, and with hard work and practice, they can accomplish successful results. Understanding and believing in the Ladder to Success is one of the most important steps and building blocks in helping young people achieve greatness.

"The Interview"

Karen read the classified ad a second time. This job was her dream of a lifetime, and it was going to be available in her hometown! She had gone away to college to prepare for this moment. She had worked for the last five years, away from home, to get the experience she needed to be in the position she was in right now. Her mind raced back to an earlier time, when her high school counselor had smiled as Karen gushed out what she hoped to do some day. Well, here it was—perhaps at her fingertips. When her husband came in from work, she couldn't wait to tell him what she felt like she should do.

"Honey, come here, and sit down. Guess what? The editor's position of my home town paper is open, and I think I should apply."

"Karen, that's great news, and I agree! This would be so perfect for you! And your journalism degree, plus working here for this newspaper as a reporter for the last few years-I think you're ready."

"But what about your job, Glen?"

"Oh, I think my boss will be flexible. As a pharmaceutical rep, I travel so much anyway, it wouldn't be that much different for me. Besides, I love your folks, and think I'd enjoy living in your home town."

"OK—that settles it. I'm going to go for it."

In the days that followed, Karen worked on her resume, filled out her application, secured her reference letters, and sent in her portfolio packet a couple of days before the deadline. She was somewhat surprised when only a week later she received a phone call from the retiring editor.

"Hi Karen, I remember you from high school. Didn't you even intern down here for a week as part of a class assignment your senior year?"

"I sure did, Mr. Daily. And I loved it."

"Well, we'd like to schedule an interview with you. We're going to sit down and talk about this position with four people, and you're in the mix. We have a couple of editors from other papers who have applied, and also someone from a large magazine in New York has expressed an interest. If it works for you, I'll put you down for 1 PM, two weeks from today. Will that work?"

"Sure will, Mr. Daily. Thank you so much for calling me and giving me this opportunity. I'll be there. See you soon."

As Karen hung up the phone, her heart sank. "Two experienced editors, and a journalist from New York?...I'll never be able to match up to that type of talent. I bet they're just doing this as a courtesy to me since I'm a hometown girl who went away to the big state university, and they want me to know they're proud of me."

Over the next few days, Karen could not get her doubts out of her mind. Glen encouraged her, and reminded her that there was no way she could control any of the other variables, except to prepare for the interview, and let the fears go.

But, she didn't let them go. Instead of thinking the best, she thought mostly the worst. Finally, on the eve of the interview, she called Mr. Daily. "I've changed my mind. Please pull my application. Let the interview team know how grateful I am to even be considered. I know you will find just the right person for this position. Thanks again."

Karen felt empowered for a few days by her decision. She felt in control. She had done the bold thing, and not pretended she could bluff her way through when she had such stiff competition.

...Until a month later, when she by coincidence ran into an old schoolmate from high school at the mall. "Karen, so glad to see you. I hear you turned down the editor's position at our newspaper back home."

"Well, not exactly. I just changed my mind on the interview. They had so many talented and more experienced applicants–even a journalist from a large magazine in New York."

"Oh, he pulled out too at the last minute. The other two did not have the total package of skills Mr. Daily was looking for, so they decided to give it to one of their young kids who's been there a year or two. Mr. Daily really wanted someone who fit his homegrown management style, and who knew the town."

As Karen walked to her car, and drove home, her stomach hurt so much she thought she was going to throw up. And she cried so much that she had to pull over twice to clear her eyes so she could see the road.

"Why didn't I try?" she scolded herself. "What did I have to lose? Now, I'll never know."

But one day, about three months later, the phone rang as Karen was headed out the door on her way to cover a story. "Karen, Mr. Daily here. Our new editor is returning to school to do graduate work. He just told me today. Could I come over and have lunch with you sometime this week?"

"Mr. Daly, when do I start! I can do that job! Thank you, thank you, thank you!"

And never again, for the rest of her life, did Karen ever pull away from an opportunity because of her fears. Because she had learned, the hard way, what it feels like to have the dream, and the opportunity to go for it, but to get scared…and then never know.

Questions for Reflection

1. Can you remember a time in your life when you quit an activity or when you ran from an opportunity due to the fear of failure?

2. What are some strategies we can use in working with kids to help them learn to face fear in the eye and chase their dreams?

3. What parts of our current system of schooling steer kids away from taking appropriate risks?

4. Share an example of an experience when you turned 'lemons into lemonade'.

In Failing Forward, *John C. Maxwell (2004) points out that there is such a fine line between success and failure, and that those who embrace their failures as opportunities to learn along the road to success have a huge advantage over those who shy away from risks due to fear of failure.*

Responsibility Builds Self-Discipline and Self-Confidence
Step 4

I am sure you have heard the statement, "Most things happen for a reason." Growing up, I never really understood why anyone would say that. However, during my college experience, I came to see the real meaning of those words.

I grew up in a very unique family situation. As a young boy, I lived in Michigan with my mother, my aunt, my grandmother, and my grandfather. Being the only child with four adults in the home provided a distinct advantage for me in terms of getting what I wanted. I quickly learned that if one person told me "no", then I would keep going until I gained approval from someone. You already know how most grandparents spoil their grandchildren. Now imagine living in the same home with them.

Also, my mother, aunt, and grandfather all worked full-time jobs. This left me to be raised for the most part by my grandmother. Over time, I developed a bond with my grandmother that resembled one that a mother and son would share.

When I was six, my grandfather retired from Ford Motor Company, and we all moved to Kentucky to our family's original home place. When I was in eighth grade, my mother got married to a former high school classmate of hers who was living in Indianapolis, Indiana. I made a decision to stay in Kentucky with my grandparents and my aunt. While it was difficult for me to see my mother move away, the decision to stay was relatively easy for me considering the bond that I had developed with my grandmother and the friendships I had made in school.

Another jolt to our family arrangement occurred during my junior year of high school, when my aunt got married and moved to Dayton, Ohio. This now left just my grandparents and me in our home. Despite the fact that she had endured open-heart surgery almost a decade earlier, my grandmother was the type of person who did everything around the house. She cooked every meal, washed all of the clothes, and she even kept up with all of the family finances.

As I approached high school graduation, I had lived a completely carefree life in which I had developed very little responsibility or self-discipline. While I was in a very loving and encouraging family atmosphere, I really had no major responsibilities other than to make sure that I performed well in school. However, I was always very competitive and self-motivated when it came to grades so that was never a big issue for me.

After examining my options, I decided to attend the University of Kentucky, which was approximately two hours away from our home. Unfortunately for me, however, I was completely unprepared to tackle the responsibilities involved in being a college student living independently away from home. When I look back, the following facts are hard for me to believe, but they are true.

When I enrolled at the University of Kentucky, I had never

washed a load of clothes in my life. I had never even written a check. As a matter fact, when I opened my checking account the summer after my high school graduation, the first check that I ever wrote was to the university. I also had never cooked a real meal. I might have made a frozen dinner once or twice, but I am sure that my grandmother was still there to oversee the project. Finally, to put the icing on the cake, I had never even driven by myself in the city of Lexington until the week that my classes started that fall!

As you can imagine, I was extremely homesick within a few days. I only knew two or three people out of the approximate 23,000 students attending UK. Most of my friends had stayed closer to home to attend college. Within my first three months, I had already decided to move back home at the end of my first semester to attend our local community college. Even though I successfully completed my courses during that first semester of college, I was completely unprepared for the responsibilities of living on my own.

I enrolled for the spring semester at our local community college, and things were pretty much back to the way they had always been. I once again had no real responsibilities. Then, the most traumatic event of my life occurred in early March of that year. I was gone one evening attending a high school basketball game. When I returned home, my grandfather told me that my grandmother had fallen and was very ill in the bed. I rushed to her side. She kept saying that she did not want to go to the hospital, but it was obvious that she was having difficulty breathing.

I called for an ambulance, and when my grandmother arrived at the hospital, we were soon informed that she had suffered a major heart attack. She was taken to Lexington to a larger hospital where her heart specialist could see her. They gave us a slim hope for her survival, and after only four days in the hospital, she died.

As long as I live, I will never forget the hopeless feeling that I endured all the way home over that long two hour drive in the back seat of a car with my grandfather and uncle. For about six months after the funeral, I was in a deep depression. Not only had I lost the most significant person in my life at that time, I also was completely overwhelmed and unsure about what to do next. My grandfather and I were in the same boat. Neither of us had ever handled any real responsibilities around our home. I had no confidence that I could manage our household.

For a while, things got worse. I didn't keep up with washing dishes and clothes as I should have. I was late on some bills that I was now responsible for writing the checks and mailing. As depressed as I was, my grandfather was in much worse condition, which made me feel even more compelled to take care of things around our home.

The harsh reality of my situation made me wake up one day and realize that I had to grasp this responsibility and conquer it. I had always been encouraged positively by my grandmother, and she had instilled in me the belief that I could accomplish anything when I set my mind to it. I started developing routines, and I quickly realized that I could manage our household.

About a year and a half later, I had completed all of my courses at the community college, and I now was prepared to tackle the responsibilities of being an independent college student. I went back to the University of Kentucky to complete my degree. After moving back to Lexington, I managed my responsibilities at my apartment in Lexington during the week, and on the weekends, I came back to handle responsibilities at our home in eastern Kentucky.

For a long time after my grandmother died, I kept asking myself why this tragedy had happened to me. However, I finally realized that I had never learned the real meaning of responsibility and self-discipline. I never would have gained the proper confidence in my abilities and been so prepared to maintain the level of responsibility necessary to be successful in life. It became apparent to me that while some things are unexplainable, most things in life do happen for a reason, even though we may not understand why for a long time.

Now that you have heard the story of how I came to understand the significance of learning responsibility, it is important to understand what this leadership trait means in the process of raising children to be successful. In my examination of the lives of several successful adults, the trait of responsibility seemed to be a very common thread among all of them.

As a matter of fact, successful businessman Bob Hutchison's

parents instilled responsibility in him at a very early age. Growing up in Ohio, Bob's parents never provided him with an allowance, as they figured chores around their home were things that should be done without being paid. He was encouraged to work for extra money if he wanted to purchase extra things for himself, but they made sure he had what he needed.

In an interview, Bob pointed out one example when his parents had given him an old baseball glove that had belonged to one of his brothers. Instead, he wanted a new glove, and his dad told him that would be fine, but he would have to pay for it. When he was just nine years old, Bob started a newspaper route in his neighborhood so he could start saving money to purchase the extra things he wanted. He rode his bicycle and delivered newspapers until he was 14 years old.

Another example of how Bob's parents helped him develop responsibility occurred in high school when they had gotten him a used car. After a short while, Bob decided he wanted a new car. Once again, his father said that would be fine. When he found the car he wanted and the sale was complete, his father reached him the payment book and told him that it was his responsibility to make sure the payments were made on time.

The price he paid for that new car was giving up most of his weekends and evenings so he could work at a local McDonald's to earn the money necessary to make his payments. Bob now points to that early development of responsibility as one of the keys to his immense success today as an owner of many McDonald's franchises and multiple car dealerships.

In looking at the lives of successful people, it appears that responsibility develops three very important traits necessary for success. Those traits are a strong work ethic, a high level of self-discipline and a sense of self-confidence. Without these three qualities, it is difficult to achieve and almost impossible to maintain any high level of success. With the understanding that developing responsibility is crucial to becoming a successful leader someday, it seems obvious that parents, grandparents, teachers, and coaches should all be finding ways to help our youth achieve high levels of responsibility.

The only question that remains is how we should effectively teach responsibility to our youth today. Does this mean that parents should send their children out on newspaper routes when they are nine years old? Even Bob Hutchison suggests that most of our neighborhoods today are not safe enough to send young people out to work in the community the way he did at such an early age.

However, many adults would agree that they often feel like their children are too young to handle much responsibility. The sad thing is that this trait is the one most likely to go missing in a lot of loving and caring households. If they could only realize that work ethic, self-discipline and self-confidence would result if the children in their lives would develop a strong sense of responsibility.

As I pointed out in the introduction, many parents do not want their children to suffer hardships. Some parents might feel guilty for working a lot and not spending enough time with their children. Still yet, other parents are busy and just feel it is easier to do things on their own rather than taking the time to allow their children to learn how to complete tasks around the house. No matter what the reason, it is obvious that we have an epidemic of children today who do not have any sense of responsibility.

This lack of responsibility is also evident today in our classrooms. Unfortunately, because of the pressures being placed on our schools to meet high stakes testing demands, most teachers have been forced to narrow the curriculum and spoon feed instruction to students so they can achieve a score on a test. In today's educational environment, students have few opportunities to develop responsibility. Today, most of the emphasis is on core subject areas, especially reading and math. Also, the curriculum has been narrowed more each year to teach items that are more likely to appear on year-end state testing.

Important programs such as character education and other enrichment activities that teach life skills have been abandoned or reduced to a minimum in most schools. At the high school level, many programs and related student organizations such as Future Business Leaders of America and Future Farmers of America have been minimized over time to allow for more testing related instruction. Unfortunately for our high school students today, these often abandoned programs are so important in developing leadership skills and responsibility.

Hopefully, our federal and state government leaders will see the critical mistakes they have made before another generation of students graduate from high school without developing leadership skills and responsibility. At an individual level, I applaud those teachers who have realized the critical importance of developing these skills and have created activities to encourage growth in these areas.

At home, parents need to let their children develop responsibility by doing things on their own. For instance, would it be that bad to let children do simple household tasks on their own, such as washing clothes or managing their own small checking or savings accounts? Of course, I have been just as guilty as the next parent in feeling that it would be so much easier to do household tasks myself, especially considering that more than likely my children would do some things incorrectly, and I would have to spend more time helping them understand their mistakes and correcting them.

The point I am making is that any time spent developing responsibility is very beneficial in helping build a child's confidence, work ethic, and self-discipline. If you think about it, how many things have you retained in life that you didn't experience on your own? It is like riding with someone to a place you have never been. Until you have driven the route yourself, it will always be hard to remember all the turns no matter how many times you have been a passenger in the past. The earlier you can help a child gain confidence through the development of responsibility and self-discipline, the better he or she will be equipped to deal with the pressures of the 21st Century.

Even though I grew up in a very loving and encouraging home, I was rarely taught any principles of responsibility as a child. My grandparents loved me so much that they did not expect me to work around the house, even though this would have helped me become more responsible. If I had not endured a terrible family tragedy in losing my grandmother, I might have never developed a high level of responsibility. If we as adults are truly concerned with helping the young people in our lives achieve success and become our future leaders, we must strive to teach them the critical leadership trait of responsibility.

"But He's My Baby!"

Jimmy's Mom went running onto the field after the game. "Coach Larson! My boy's just ten years old! Don't you think he should have kept pitching those last three innings? After all, he's who got you to this playoff anyway!"

"Nellie, Jimmy played a great game—as always. But I wanted one of my older boys pitching the last few innings in this one. Experience means a lot, and the fact that Jimmy even started today is a testament to how well he's played all year. Take him home, and enjoy the rest of the summer. Aren't you glad we won this one? This is the first league championship for the Reds in the last ten years!"

"What do you mean take him home? He's on the All Star team isn't he? Aren't they supposed to practice here in a few minutes?"

"Nellie, at our coach's meeting last night, we decided we should limit the All Stars to the eleven and twelve year olds. So, next year, I'd imagine Jimmy will be on the team."

"That's discrimination Coach Larson! You and I both know that Jimmy's one of the best players in this league, and certainly the best ten year old. Surely you all know you'll need him on the All Star team if you expect to win anything in the tournament next week."

"Yes, Jimmy is awfully good for his age. But we have many other boys who are also very skilled players. I think we'll do just fine. And I really do think it's more fair to limit the All Star team to the older boys."

"Well that's just great, then, Coach. I'll have you know that you've coached your last game with my little Jim. We'll be going to another league next year—across town. One of the coaches over there has already promised me that Jimmy would play more than you've played him. So, good luck next year when you're looking around for my kid to pull you through."

"I hope you will think this through, Nellie. Jimmy has played on this team for two years now, and these are his schoolmates too. I'd hate to see him pulled out of our league at this juncture."

"You should have thought of that when you voted for your stupid rule that excluded him from the All Star team, coach!...I've gotta go. Have a good life!"

"Yes Ma'm. Has been nice working with Jimmy, Nellie. He's a fine young man. I do hope to see him next spring at our first practice."

Jimmy had been standing at the concession stand nearby, eating a hot dog and drinking a Coke. He had heard the entire conversation, and cried while sitting in the back of the car on the way home.

"I don't want to change leagues, Mom! I like Coach Larson, and my teammates. It's OK if I don't play on the All Stars this summer. I promise—it's no big deal."

"It's a big deal to me Jimmy. If you're going to play high school ball, and then go on to college on a baseball scholarship, we're not letting coaches treat you this way...Now, let's drive over to

Southtown, and find that coach who told me he needed you. Perhaps they have a game or two left in their season."

"Mom, please no. Besides, I promised Papaw I'd mow his grass for the rest of the summer—just as soon as my ball season was over."

"No, no, no. Papaw can mow his own lawn. He never ceases to amaze me—always wanting you to come over to his house and work. You're just a little boy, and I'll decide when you're old enough to work, James Daniel. Not Papaw!"

"But Mom—I like to work. I know how to pour gas in Papaw's mower now, and next time he told me he had some other chores I could help with. Going over there is one of the most fun things I do all summer. In fact, I'd like to spend a week with he and Mamaw if that's alright with you. He told me after we got our morning work done, he'd take me fishing a couple of times."

"No, it's not OK with me. You're too young to be hanging out at your grandparents for a week away from home. Much too young…Now, let's find that other coach and then get you home. You're probably exhausted after that game. I'll stop by the 'dairy barn' and get you a shake, and then you need to get to bed and take a nap. You look overheated to me."

Questions for Reflection

1. In school or at home, what are some ways you help the kids you mentor to learn appropriate responsibility?

2. What are other examples of how adults can accidentally impede the healthy developmental progress of children?

3. What is your philosophy regarding children and youth doing chores at home?

4. When you were growing up, when did you first notice that you were able to take care of yourself independently?

5. Can we "love" a child so much that we handicap him/her in being well prepared for the various stages of life? Is this a mature love, or a selfish love?

In The 5 Patterns of Extraordinary Careers, *James M. Citrin and Richard A. Smith (2003) define key tendencies and habits of people who are successful. Fulfillment in life does not happen by chance.*

Attitude Will Determine Your Altitude
Step 5

Of all the leadership traits discussed in this book, attitude is definitely among the most crucial factors in determining one's level of success. I know you could be thinking this may not be as true anymore, considering some of the stories about ruthless tycoons who have accumulated great wealth over the past century. However, the old top-down style of business management is quickly becoming a thing of the past. As we discussed in Step 2, managing through fear is no longer a highly effective way of achieving peak performance.

As businessmen and entrepreneurs have discovered that maintaining an encouraging attitude and climate in the workplace can lead to greater levels of success, this type of positive leadership has swept rapidly through the business world. Autocratic leaders with poor attitudes are becoming obsolete because the most talented people now have better choices when searching for the right job.

This does not mean the world is free of people with bad attitudes. There will always be some managers who want to rule with an iron fist. Also, there will always be those people who are so talented in an area that they can still succeed even though they have a bad attitude. I am sure you can think of famous actors, musicians, or athletes who do not have a great attitude but still maintain a high level of success in their field because of their enormous talent.

However, when looking at the whole population, these people are far and few between. This also leads to a larger question. What is the true definition of success? Unfortunately, most people only define success in terms of money and material possessions. But this is only one piece of the success puzzle, and not often the most important.

Sure, not having money can severely limit a person's opportunities to experience joy and success. However, people quickly forget about the importance of having successful relationships. These positive connections come both in the form of dating and marriage, but should also exist with friendly interpersonal bonds. The human spirit craves close relationships with others. Most happy people have both types of relationships in their lives, but it is crucial to have some type of interpersonal connections with others.

This healthy balance in life is necessary to experience true success and happiness. By focusing on balance, one can maintain a great career and strong work ethic while enjoying close interpersonal relationships with others. The key to establishing this balance is attitude. By carrying a positive attitude, a person will attract and maintain relationships with other people who have positive attitudes. Also, a good attitude leads to greater self-confidence which definitely has a positive effect on career success.

In his book, The Difference Maker, John Maxwell breaks down

the importance of attitude. In describing attitude, he says, "It makes you or breaks you. It lifts you up or brings you down. A positive mental attitude will not let you do everything. But it can help you do anything better than you would if your attitude were negative."

If simply carrying a positive attitude can help lead to success, then why is this principle so hard to master? The answer lies in our development as we grow up through childhood and into adolescence. As we discussed in earlier chapters, two of the biggest obstacles getting in the way of achieving success are developing a fear of failure and continually concentrating on our weaknesses instead of our strengths or talent areas.

I have observed that little children tend to believe they can do almost anything, but by the time they are nine or ten years old, most of them have developed a negative self-image, at least in some areas. By having a negative concept of failure and thinking of it as something we should always try to avoid, we actually encourage our children to be pessimistic and believe things will go wrong if they attempt something new. Before long, this can grow into a negative attitude, at least in the area of self-confidence.

The other issue is our society's focus on improving weaknesses. It is common sense that we feel higher levels of self-confidence in our areas of strength or talent. Likewise, we have lower levels of self-confidence in our areas of weakness. By neglecting strengths and focusing more attention on constantly improving weaknesses, children quickly become less confident and eventually develop more of a negative attitude and believe they are failures, or at best they just feel very ordinary.

This does not mean that children should never work in their areas of weakness. Some weaknesses are very important to improve and will require some work. However, every child deserves to feel confident and should develop pride in their areas of talent. The leadership trait of having a positive attitude and a high level of self-confidence can go a long way in determining the success of our children.

The last issue surrounding the development of a positive attitude in our children is modeling. I try to remember that the old adage, "Do as I say, not as I do," does not work with children. They may try to fake it in front of you, but ultimately, most children will model the behavior they observe in their parents, teachers, coaches, and other significant people in their lives. This is a very difficult fact for many of us to swallow, but when we display a negative attitude about something, there is a great chance our children will follow suit and mimic the same attitude.

On the flip side, children have a much greater capacity to be successful when they are met with positive attitudes and are encouraged to work harder when they encounter failure. Also, children who are always praised for their areas of talent tend to show a greater desire to work harder in those areas. This results in a higher level of self-confidence and a positive attitude.

Perhaps the greatest example of how a positive attitude can help determine a person's success is Nick Vujicic. Because of a rare birth disorder, Vujicic was born with no arms and no legs. Despite having perfectly normal mental and cognitive development, he was not allowed at first to attend a mainstream school where he lived in Australia. However, laws soon changed, and he was provided the opportunity to attend a regular school.

While this disability would be completely overwhelming to most people, Vujicic developed a positive attitude early in his life. Even though some other children teased and made fun of him as a young child, he decided that he was going to prove to others that he could be successful and be an inspiration to anyone who might have a negative self-image. Even though he has no arms or legs, he was born with two small feet, one of which has two toes. He worked hard to learn how to move around and eventually learned to write with his foot. He learned how to kick a ball, answer a phone, and amazingly enough, he can type 43 words per minute on a computer.

Unfortunately, most people with a disability of this magnitude would have given up on having a successful career. Instead, Vujicic's positive attitude turned this major obstacle into an opportunity as he has spoken live to countless people around the world, and has appeared on multiple television programs, including 20/20 and The Oprah Winfrey Show. As a successful motivational speaker, Vujicic spreads his message that 'Attitude is altitude' and, 'You should never give up' to children and adults around the world. Vujicic is a fabulous example of how attitude can make the difference in achieving success.

Another example of someone achieving success in the face of adversity through a positive attitude is Ervin Magic Johnson. Johnson was one of ten children and definitely did not live with a silver spoon in his mouth as a child. He attended a high school in Flint, Michigan that had experienced some racial tensions because of desegregation in the 1970's. However, Magic kept his patented smile on his face and crossed racial barriers to make friends at Everett High School. He combined his positive attitude and amazing talent as a basketball player to lead Everett to a state championship his senior season.

Magic then accepted a scholarship to play for Michigan State University, where he only stayed two seasons, culminating with an NCAA basketball championship in 1979. He was then selected first in the 1979 NBA draft by the Los Angeles Lakers. In his first season in the NBA, Magic led the Lakers to an NBA championship by scoring 42 points, grabbing 15 rebounds, and dishing out seven assists in the series clinching sixth game. This completed an amazing run where Magic had won a high school, collegiate, and professional basketball championship in a span of only four years.

The success definitely did not end there for Magic, as he went on to win a total of five NBA titles, three Most Valuable Player awards, and twelve All-Star Game selections. His positive attitude and talent had carried him to heights greater than most people could ever imagine. However, before the start of the 1991-92 season,

Magic received earth shattering news when he learned that he had tested positive for HIV (Human Immunodeficiency Virus). At the time of his infliction, HIV and AIDS had reached a panic stage, and many people were afraid to come into human contact with an HIV positive person.

Magic was one of the first, and perhaps the most well known celebrity to ever test positive for HIV. He was immediately forced to retire from the NBA, and fans everywhere were completely numbed by this apparent tragedy. Since there was no known cure for HIV, it seemed certain that we would watch this popular celebrity and athlete become weak and die from AIDS right before our eyes.

But this is where Magic's positive attitude may have made the greatest difference not only for him, but for HIV afflicted people around the world. Instead of giving up like many people might do when faced with seemingly insurmountable odds of recovery, Magic aggressively fought the disease. Now, over two decades later, Magic is still standing strong as a successful businessman and a huge advocate in the fight against HIV and AIDS.

From a personal standpoint, I have always believed that even though you cannot change the events that occur in your life, you can always adjust your attitude to make the best of any situation. In essence, what could be a tragedy to one person can wind up being a constructive event for another person because of having a positive attitude.

At the first sign of distress, many people allow negative attitudes and fear to consume them, instead of maintaining a positive attitude and searching for successful solutions to situations. Nick Vujicic and Magic Johnson are clear examples of how having a good attitude can lead to positive outcomes and success.

"I Could Have Been Him"

Ellen got the call while rocking her baby to sleep, and just getting ready to help her elderly father with his lunch. Her hands quivered as she hung up the phone.

"What is it baby girl?" Her father could tell something was wrong.

"Oh, nothing Dad. Jay's coming home early from work, and I need to go give him a ride. Can you watch Ethan for an hour or so?"

"Sure thing. The little guy and me will be fine. You run along and I'll see you when you get back. We'll be right here—watching our afternoon 'soaps'."

Ellen wiped tears from her eyes as she tried to see the road. This was not the first time Jay had done this. When he got in the car, and slammed the door, Ellen pointed her finger at him, and simply said, "Shut up and listen…or I'm going to drive this car right downtown to the bus station, and buy you a one way ticket. Do you understand me?"

"But Ellen, let me explain. It's my boss. He's on me all the time. He knows he's got me doing menial tasks when with my degree I should already be managing other people. But, no-o-o, he's got to be Mister Big Man, Mister 'Do As I Say'. So, this morning, I simply told him he needed to take a good look at his attitude, and the next thing I knew, they were giving me severance pay. I'm finding a lawyer. I ain't taking this crap! Who does he think he is, anyway? He ain't no leader. In fact, I should be him—in charge of our department. I could do it with my hands tied behind my back, and blindfolded!"″

"See Jay, that's' just what I mean. Honey, you haven't even worked there three months yet! And you're telling your supervisor that he has an attitude problem?"

"But he does, Ellen. He's a jerk."

"Ok, Jay. I've let you plead your case. Now, put on your seatbelt, and listen…When you and I first got married, you had just lost an academic scholarship to one of the top schools in the country. We'll be paying on that loan we borrowed to get you through school for a long, long time. Then there was that thing that cost us a couple of hundred because you refused to return a phone call to the bank while we were on our honeymoon."

"But…"

"I'm not finished Jay. A short time later, you landed a real good job in your field of study and I thought you were learning. But nope, ol' Jay always has to approach life with an attitude. So, next thing I know, you're home again—drawing unemployment. And the next two jobs, it was the same thing. It's been three years Jay, and you've been home more than you've been employed."

"But they were singling me out Babe—making me do work the janitor could do!"

"So–big deal. I'm a school teacher, and I do custodial work all the time Jay. If it needs to get done, sometimes, we just swallow our pride, and do it."

"Not me."

"That's right—not you. You'd rather leave me and the baby home with no clue as to how we're going to pay the bills, and leave me an emotional wreck all the time, than to admit that you have a problem and need help."

"Need help?"

"Yes, need help!"

"What's that supposed to mean?"

"It means you can't hold a job Jay! It means you can't see two feet in front of your face. It means your attitude is pulling this whole family down. So, thanks to you losing yet another golden opportunity to be gainfully employed, I'm going to have to go back to my school this fall and ask to work in the after-school tutoring program, and anything else they'll pay me to do—just to somehow make ends meet. It's not fair Jay! You're killing me…you're killing our family…you're destroying your career. Can't you see the reality of it all?"

"Oh yeah, I see the reality alright. I see you whining and bellyaching on your summer break, taking care of your ol' man and not even trying to have some sympathy for me during this very stressful time where I have been wronged at work."

"You've not been wronged at work, Jay! You've been wronging the people you work with, and even the people at home you say you love. Your attitude stinks Jay! You're so self-centered I don't know anyone who wants to be around you anymore!"

Jay stubbed up, and looked out the window as Ellen drove toward home. But then, she made a sudden exit off the freeway, and pulled into the bus station.

"It's the end of the line for me, Jay. You have two choices. You can catch a ride on a bus and don't come home until you are ready to face life with a smile, and a willingness to work through the difficulties of what each day might bring. Or, you can take a taxi to a counselor and take a real good look inside. Here's thirty bucks. It's all I have. Now get out, and grow up—or don't come back home. I've got to go to the bank and take out another loan. Then I've got to get home and take care of our kid and my dad...It's called life Jay. I don't know if you've ever figured that out."

Questions for Reflection

1. Can you think of someone you know who has struggled with an attitude problem, thus throwing away opportunities that were there for the taking?

2. Why do you think some people seem to get all the breaks in life and are always considered lucky?

3. Can you think of someone you know who has risen above various issues to live an impacting and fulfilling life? What seems to be their formula for success?

4. What types of people do you enjoy being around?

5. What types of people would you rather not spend time with on a regular basis?

6. What are the attitudes of your children or your students, and how does their attitude affect their success?

In The Fred Factor, *Mark Sanborn (2002) illustrates the power of one person approaching work and life with a great attitude and concern for others. Thus, the ordinary becomes the extraordinary…the mundane becomes a special experience.*

Cultivating Positive Communication Skills
Step 6

Up to this point, we have been exploring how attitude, talent, motivation, and responsibility are at the heart of leadership. If you are on board with the importance of these skills, then you are ready to open the door to access these leadership traits. The key to unlocking that door is communication.

Unfortunately, few people ever master positive communication skills. After examining this puzzling truth, I think the primary reason for this problem is that many people do not completely understand how communication actually works. Perhaps the biggest myth with communication is that we all tend to think that if we say something, then others will understand what we are saying. This leads to the general perception that communication can be a one-way street. So many people feel that if they have said something, their intended audience will receive the exact message that was intended, but this rarely happens in real life.

This is where feedback comes into play. The first key to understanding how communication works is to accept that communication is always a two-way street. As a matter of fact, communication cannot occur properly without a message and feedback. So often, we have a thought or an idea, but when we try to convey that message, the recipients may gather a completely different meaning from our words than we actually intended.

There are actually so many different factors that can alter our communication attempts. First of all, tone can be a huge factor in sending and receiving messages. For example, the exact same phrase can have completely opposite meanings just because of differences in our tone. If I learn that my favorite team just won a big game, and I say, "That's great," in an upbeat tone, others will see that I am happy. On the other hand, if I learn that my team just lost a big game, and I say, "That's great," in a real sarcastic or negative tone, others will see that I am unhappy with the results. Either way, I said the exact same words, but with two entirely different meanings.

Non-verbal communication can also alter the meaning of an intended message. For instance, if a coach is upset at the actions of one of his players, and he says, "Come on," with a frown on his face while dropping his head, the nonverbal cues can send a message that he is unhappy. However, if the same coach says, "Come on," with a look of enthusiasm on his face while waving the player toward him, the nonverbal cues can send a message that he is happy with the efforts of the player.

Now, I hope you are beginning to see how confusing our attempts at communication can be at times. It is clear that words alone do not mean anything unless they are received with the exact meaning that we intend when we speak them. This is also true with written words. Even though it is harder to convey tone and feelings at times in our written words, the way we phrase what we write can greatly change the message that is conveyed. Including words like "please" and "thank you" can help send a positive tone, while making command statements and using all capital letters or exclamation points can sometimes send a negative tone.

The other side to positive communication is understanding feedback. Unless you have clear feedback, it is impossible to know if your message was received the way you intended it. Feedback also comes in a variety of methods, including tone and non-verbal cues.

For instance, as you say something, you can often look at facial expressions to see how your audience is receiving your message. You can also see if there are verbal responses with different tones. Often great leaders will ask for feedback by asking questions such as, "Do you think this idea will work?" The most successful people seem to have a mastery of positive communication skills, including a good understanding of feedback.

When trying to look at examples of how communication skills can help determine a leader's success, one needs to look no further than the 40th President of the United States, Ronald Reagan. As a matter of fact, Reagan was nicknamed "The Great Communicator." Reagan began his career as a radio announcer and later became an actor. He had roles in many films during his career and eventually hosted the "General Electric Theatre" on television. During this time in his career, he used his communication skills to pursue leadership roles as he was elected president of the Screen Actors Guild for a total of seven years.

After his acting career, Reagan was elected as governor of California for two terms, extending from 1967-1975. Then, in 1980, he was elected President of the United States. He was elected for two terms, as he stayed in office from 1981-1989.

Even though America faced difficult economic times when he took office, Reagan used his outstanding communication skills to make the American public feel secure and confident in what the future would hold. He increased nationalism and pride by rallying Americans through messages of anti-Communism.

One of Reagan's greatest accomplishments was ending the "Cold War", as he gave a famous speech in Germany targeted at Soviet leader Mikhail Gorbachev. He exclaimed, "Mr. Gorbachev, tear down this wall," referring to the Berlin Wall that separated communist controlled East Germany from West Germany. Two years after his speech in 1989, the Berlin Wall was torn down and the Soviet Union eventually collapsed. Reagan and Gorbachev also held multiple nuclear summits resulting in an arms reduction treaty that also helped to end the "Cold War."

During his second term in office, Reagan encountered a huge controversy that could have tainted his entire presidency. A secret weapons agreement that when exposed became the Iran-Contra scandal caused many to question Reagan and others in his administration. Weapons were secretly sold to Iran in return for efforts to release American hostages. Some of this money was diverted to fund Contra militants in Honduras, even though

Congress had passed laws prohibiting this activity.

However, Reagan's superior communication skills and great rapport with the American public allowed him to quickly overcome the negative attention surrounding this event. Reagan is now considered one of the greatest American presidents, and one of the primary reasons for his success was his ability to communicate so effectively.

Just to make sure that this example of positive communication skills does not become a partisan debate, I will share another example of a leader who had a gift when it came to relating with the American public. Bill Clinton, who served as our 42nd President, clearly had a gift for communicating that is nearly unmatched among leaders in the current era.

During his presidency, Clinton had an affair with a twenty-two-year-old intern named Monica Lewinsky. He denied the allegations at first and eventually became only the second President of the United States to be impeached. However, he was later acquitted on both charges of perjury and obstruction of justice.

Even though Clinton had been tagged with the nickname "Slick Willie" earlier in his political career, his outstanding communication skills allowed him to shake off any negative publicity and actually gave him a positive image with most Americans. Clinton's moderate policies and appeal to both conservative and liberal voters allowed him to be elected to two terms of office. He presided over one the longest periods of economic growth in American history.

While many people questioned his moral compass, no one can question his overwhelming ability to communicate. Despite some controversial activities during his eight years in office, Clinton's ability to relate positively with the American public propelled him to a high approval rating when he left office. Actually, both Reagan and Clinton left office with 60 percent or higher approval ratings which are among the very best of the modern era.

Both Reagan and Clinton are fantastic examples of how great communication skills can help build favorable relationships with others. Not only did both men leave office with high approval ratings, they each used their strong ability to communicate to overcome negative situations that would have ruined many leaders' careers.

It is important to note that having great communication skills alone will not always result in positive leadership, unless other principles described in this book are applied. Many people fall victim to scams everyday because imposters with good communication skills intentionally mislead and swindle others

One of the most impacting examples of improper use of communication is Adolf Hitler. As leader of Germany after World War I, Hitler used his outstanding communication skills to captivate the German people during a time of depression and despair. He evoked feelings of pride and nationalism from many Germans, and he inspired them to commit terrible acts of human cruelty toward Jews and other minority groups. Countless people were murdered as a result of Hitler's exceptional ability to communicate, which he used for evil purposes.

Hitler is one of many political leaders who have used savvy communication skills to persuade others to follow questionable agendas. Today, gang leaders and drug dealers often use great communication skills to persuade young people to make destructive decisions. This is yet another reason why it is vital that we teach positive communication skills in conjunction with other leadership principles, so our young people can make the right decisions when encountered with negative peer pressure.

So far in this chapter, we have focused primarily on public forms of communication. These public speaking skills are essential for most people to become highly successful in life. Even though there are some exceptions of introverts who become successful, the vast majority of high achievers in life have great communication skills.

However, public speaking is only part of this process. Interpersonal communication skills are just as important to one's future success as public speaking skills. As a matter of fact, interpersonal skills may be more important in many areas. The ability to relate well to others in one-on-one situations is vital in building trust and respect in the workplace.

As we discussed in Step 2, the 'old school' model of management based on fear has quickly faded from today's business world. Instead, being able to relate positively to others is one of the most important skills in climbing up the Ladder to Success.

In addition to helping one become a high achiever in the world of work, good interpersonal skills are also critical to building strong bonds with others on a personal level. As we stated at the beginning of this book, our focus is on raising children who become successful and happy adults. It is crucial that we do not forget the importance of fulfillment and being "happy", because there are many people who achieve some measure of financial wealth but lead relatively unhappy lives.

Remember that achieving complete success not only means accomplishing career goals, but also means discovering personal happiness. There are many components that help one reach personal happiness, but one of the most important is building strong interpersonal relationships with others.

According to author John Ortberg, "The presence of rich, deep, joy-producing, life-changing, meaningful relationships is a key to happiness."

For those people who feel that money and material possessions are the key to their happiness, they need to understand that close interpersonal relationships are the actual key to happiness. If you think about this, it should make perfect sense. How many things in life are very enjoyable if you cannot share them with other people who are close to you?

Now if developing positive communication skills can make a difference in achieving both career success and personal happiness, then it should be clear that we need to make this a focal point for developing leadership skills in our youth today. Great leaders generally have a good combination of public speaking and interpersonal communication skills. The question is how to best encourage the growth and development of positive communication skills in our youth.

One area where we can help is to encourage as many public speaking opportunities as possible for the young people in our lives. This is one area where it is much better to start very early in life. Most small children have no fear of getting in front of others, but by the time children reach middle school age, they are so self-conscience and easily embarrassed that many refuse to ever get in front of others.

If the child in your life is reluctant about getting in front of others, then it is important to find something that he or she is passionate about and encourage participation in that activity. Various sports, dance teams, singing, or other extracurricular activities may be the answer. By the high school level, student organizations and clubs can often provide opportunities to build communication skills.

This is also an area where it is important to change our children's perception of failure and make sure they view it as a tool for achieving success. The more cooperative and team-building activities that we provide for young people, the better their communication skills will develop.

Social activity and adequate time playing with friends at an early age are very important in building interpersonal skills. The earlier children learn to share and work together, the quicker they can develop positive interpersonal communication skills. However, helping children obtain these skills is harder today than ever. First of all, providing opportunities for young people to participate in activities that place them in front of others requires adults to alter their busy work schedules. Many parents feel they are too busy to make time for their children to participate in a variety of activities, such as sports, dance, gymnastics, and music lessons.

Another obstacle in helping our children develop positive communication skills is the sea of technology they enjoy today. Many children do not display the desire to participate in activities outside of their homes when they have video game systems and the Internet to surf on their personal computers. When you couple this with the busy schedules of most adults today, it is easy to see why many parents do not push their children very hard to participate in extracurricular activities, especially when their children do not beg to participate. If you do not take anything else from this chapter, please understand there is absolutely no substitute for having children participate in extracurricular activities to build positive communication skills. Even though it is often so much easier to allow video games, television, and computers to serve as babysitters for our children, it is important to provide a balance where they can spend time enjoying technology while still participating in activities outside of the home.

"Why Didn't I Just Say What I Was Feeling Inside?"

Shawn had overslept, and hurriedly threw on a coat and tie as he ran to his mom's car with a glass of orange juice in one hand and an envelope in the other.

"Shawn, we're ten minutes late. Do the directions indicate a shortcut through town?"

"Nope. Sorry Mom. I forgot to set my alarm. But, I think I've got this locked up anyway. The counselor at school said the university was looking for guys like me for this new program."

"I know Shawn, but Honey, this is an interview. So, it's not a done deal…Did you go over your notes on what they might be asking?"

"No, I just figure if it is meant to be, it is meant to be."

"Shawn, you sure do have a lot of confidence for an eighteen-year-old who has no clue how he is going to afford college yet. I hope you know what you're doing, 'cause this would be such an opportunity. And, it might allow your father to quit his moonlighting job. After putting your two older siblings through school, he's getting a little tired of the sixteen hour days, don't you think?"

"Yea, Pop does seem a little run down. I'll do my best, Mom. Don't worry–piece of cake."

Shawn's mother shook her head as he dashed from the car into the admission office. She had managed to get him there with a couple of minutes to spare, but he would still be cutting it too close if the interview was in another building. He had not remembered where he was to report to—so he followed a hunch and went to the only office he had visited before. When his mom saw him dart out the back door and sprint across the main lawn of the campus, she shook her head and prayed.

"Come in Shawn, and have a seat. You seem out of breath."

"I am so sorry I'm late-a mix up at home this morning." "Oh, were you late? Another applicant just left out this other door, and we didn't know who was next. We're interviewing five candidates today, and will award three scholarships."

Shawn wished to himself that he had not blurted out his tardiness, and also was surprised that the interview was not just a formality. He wondered why he had not read the info packet more closely.

"To get us started Shawn, tell us why you are interested in this major, and how you have prepared for it."

"I don't know. I guess I just have always had such respect for your school, and also, I need to help my parents with the tuition if I am to go to an expensive place like this." (Shawn scolded himself, "What a dumb answer!").

"I see...Tell us Shawn, what do you see yourself doing in five years?"

"Oh, I don't know—hopefully making a nice salary, driving a nice car, living in an apartment on my own."

"Uh, no, we mean—your life, your career?"

"Oh yeah, that." Shawn laughed, hoping the committee would pick up on his feeble attempt to pose as a cute teenage charm. They did not, as no one smiled or gestured that he was doing fine with the interview. He cleared his throat, and realized he was in deep water already.

"Frankly Sir, I hope to make a difference. With your program training me these next four years, I know I would be well prepared."

"Tell us more about our program. How much do you know about it?"

Shawn was yet again caught off guard. "Well, uh, I know that two of my friends at school have older brothers who go here, and they say this place is awesome."

The interview was over much sooner than Shawn had assumed it would be, and he was a little surprised when escorted to the front door that no one told him he'd be getting a congratulatory letter in the mail in a few days. In fact, no one on the interview team said much of anything. They just smiled and shook his hand as he tried with his body language to plead, "Please ask me more questions. I am so ready now!" He had not begun to share what he was really thinking.

Back in the car with his mom, Shawn slammed his fist on the dashboard. "Oh Mom, I might have just blown it big time!"

"Oh now Honey, settle down. I know how you always rise to the occasion. I'm sure they saw your charm, your wit, your intelligence. Why would they not want you to be one of their scholars the next four years?"

"Oh, I'm sure they'll take our money if I choose to go here. I'm just not sure I'll be offered the scholarship."

Shawn's mom slowed down, and her voice was quivering. "Why? What did you say that would change their minds?"

"That's just it—I didn't say much of anything!"

"But Shawn, you have so wanted this scholarship. What is your heart telling you about this opportunity?"

"It's telling me that this is my moment in time. This is my chance to chase my dream to do something really special with my talents, and make a contribution to society that could be far-reaching. It's telling me that I'll do whatever it takes to study hard, make sacrifices, work a part-time job, do internships abroad—whatever my professors ask of me I'll do it. I just ask for the opportunity." Shawn looked out the window and felt an ache in the pit of his stomach.

"Honey, you didn't tell them that?"

"Nope."

"Why?"

"I don't know. I just assumed that they wanted to meet me and that would be it. I just assumed I would not need to convey my heart."

"Honey, it's always about conveying your heart. That's what

separates the men from the boys. You must share your passion with the others in the room when you're trying to communicate a message that's important."

"Turn around."

"What?"

"Turn around Mom!"

"Why?"

"'Cause I realize it may be too late. But, just maybe it's not. I'm going back to that office, and back to that interview room, and I'm going to beg them to let me share what I just shared with you."

Shawn's mother turned the car around, wondering why on this day, of all days, her son had somehow forgotten to communicate his vision. So, so much weighed in the balance.

Questions for Reflection

1. Can you remember a special time in your life when you needed to communicate just the right message, and you somehow could not articulate that message?

2. How did you feel later after the opportunity had passed?

3. Why is it important to be both a good listener and also a good communicator of what's on your mind?

4. What does it mean to 'speak from the heart'?

5. What role does preparation play in an interview, or in other situations when your thoughts and words need to be focused and specific?

6. Do you feel as though your children or students express themselves well to others?

7. Do you actively provide opportunities for your children or students to speak in front of others in both small and large group settings?

John Maxwell (2010), in Everyone Communicates, Few Connect, *reveals the reality that too few people understand. We can be talking, and in conversation — but still not connecting with the other person. The connection emotionally and relationally is the key, and takes the effectiveness of our communication to a whole new level.*

Foster a Competitive Spirit
Step 7

While building positive communication skills is a no-brainer to nearly everyone, the topic of this chapter has often gathered misconceptions from many people in recent years. A half-century ago, being highly competitive was valued as a positive trait. However, over the past couple of decades, this belief has slowly eroded. Now, a competitive spirit is often viewed with a negative connotation and is often discouraged in our youth.

Many psychologists and educational experts today believe that all children need to constantly experience feelings of success. It is thought by many scholars that any hint of losing can destroy self-confidence. This type of thinking has led to many competitive activities being removed from our schools. This trend is not limited to just athletic and physical education activities. Many competitive activities and games related to academics have also been limited so no students are deemed winners or losers.

Unfortunately, those competitive activities serve an important purpose in helping our young people develop leadership skills. Keep in mind that it is a very noble and worthwhile line of thinking to want our children to develop positive self-images. However, the negative consequences of preventing our kids from ever losing and experiencing failure far outweigh any benefits to taking this approach. If you reflect back to Step 3, we learned about the Ladder to Success, which illustrates how a positive outlook about failure can help us achieve success. The key to helping young people achieve success through competition is to help them understand that failure is only one step away from success.

Developing an internal drive to compete and succeed is one of the most important qualities that a young person needs in order to achieve long-term success. One thing I have learned through my career in education is that the older a person becomes, the harder it is to develop a competitive drive. It is important to understand that a healthy competitive drive is the fuel that propels individuals and teams to succeed in any endeavor. It could be something as simple as deciding you want to lose ten pounds, or as complex as deciding you want to win a marathon or be the CEO of a major corporation.

These are all examples of self-motivated competitions where individuals set goals to achieve a personal victory. Some people might not view losing ten pounds as a competitive event, but it is a personal competition in which individuals compete against themselves to achieve a goal.

Why is competition so important to achieving success? The answer to this question lies in the feelings of joy that all humans experience when victory is achieved. I am sure that everyone has had the opportunity to experience the pure joy of victory. I like to call it a "natural high" because it changes our entire mood and evokes feelings of pleasure and happiness. As a matter of fact, many people enjoy this feeling so much that when they are not personally engaged in a competition, they will cheer on their favorite team as a fan.

Most likely, you have cheered on your favorite sports team, whether it is professional, college, or even a local high school team. If you have ever become very involved as a fan during a game, and your team achieved victory, I am sure you have experienced the feelings of euphoria that come with winning a competition.

In a 2010 article in Newsweek titled, "Can the Saints Really Save New Orleans? How a Super Bowl Victory Could Enhance the Health of a City," two different researchers outlined the positive and often stress-relieving benefits of rooting your team on to victory. Just cheering for your favorite team can create a positive rush, leading to the body's release of endorphins which evoke feelings of pleasure. However, a victory can have even greater effects, including an increased feeling of confidence.

Now, if just cheering for your favorite team can create such a feeling of joy, imagine the feeling of euphoria that one gains from being personally invested in a competition and achieving victory. The key to the previous statement is the word, "invested." If you completely invest your heart into a competition, you will greatly increase your chances of achieving success. Also, the more effort and desire you place into a competition, the higher levels of excitement and euphoria you will enjoy upon victory. It is important to understand there is a direct relationship between your level of investment in a competition and your likelihood for success.

This understanding of how our minds and bodies work goes back to the Ladder to Success once again. Just as I described the feelings of euphoria and pure joy that come with victory, the opposite will occur for many who experience losing. Many negative emotions flow through people when they lose, including anger, sadness, and even depression. The key to how strong those negative emotions affect us is completely dependent on how much we are emotionally invested in a particular competitive activity.

For instance, I will share a personal story that still haunts me today as I watch the beginning of any NCAA basketball tournament game. If you are even a mild college basketball fan, I am sure that you are familiar with the last second Christian Laetner shot that lifted Duke to a one-point overtime victory over Kentucky in the 1992 NCAA tournament. Many basketball experts still argue today that this was the greatest NCAA game ever played.

However, if you ask a true Kentucky basketball fan about this game, you will be hard pressed to find even one who would express positive feelings about it. As a matter of fact, most UK fans could quickly tell you how disgusted they become when that shot by Laetner is replayed during the introductory song before the start of every NCAA tournament game.

Now, imagine being a student at the University of Kentucky in 1992 when the game was played. I still proclaim today that I experienced the greatest swing in emotions of my entire life that night. There were fourteen UK fans, including me, crowded into a friend's apartment in Lexington that evening. Kentucky was not expected to even come close to defeating the top-ranked Duke team that was trying to win back-to-back NCAA championships.

At one point early in the second half, I recall that UK was down by 12 points. At this time, my friends and I were prepared for a loss, and we had not invested much emotion into the game. Of course we were a little disappointed at that time, but by no means were we angry or extremely sad.

Then all of a sudden, the craziness began for us in that apartment on that fateful evening. After trailing by double-digits, Kentucky slowly started making a comeback. As the game inched closer to the end, UK pulled even and eventually forced overtime. Throughout the last few minutes before overtime, all of us in the apartment crowded within five feet of the television set as if we could get closer to Philadelphia where the actual game was being played.

We became so emotionally involved by this point that every ounce of energy we had was poured into cheering the Wildcats on to victory. As the overtime period wound down, UK point guard Sean Woods banked in a shot to give Kentucky a one-point lead with only two seconds remaining in the game. Duke called a timeout, and during those two minutes, my friends and I were on a completely natural high as we screamed with excitement and hugged each other.

I can honestly say today that when Woods' shot went through the basket, it was one of the greatest moments of pure joy that I can ever remember experiencing. The fact that all of us had invested so much emotion into this game made the thought of this victory so exciting and fulfilling. We were so happy with the apparent victory that during the timeout, we even discussed our plans for booking a trip to Minneapolis, Minnesota for the Final Four the next weekend to watch Kentucky play for a national championship.

Then, the unthinkable happened. Duke's Grant Hill threw a pass the length of the court to Laetner, who turned around and sunk a shot at the buzzer to hand Kentucky a devastating one-point loss. When the shot fell through the hoop, there was an eerie silence that could almost be felt throughout the city of Lexington for a moment. Then, all of us in the apartment were overcome with feelings of extreme anger, as if someone had stolen our most precious possession right from our fingertips.

I was so angry that I picked up a large chair that I normally would not have been able to lift by myself and threw it several feet across the room. Several of my friends also threw things or punched the wall. The feelings of anger were immediately followed by an overwhelming sense of sadness and depression. We went to eat at an Applebee's after the game and you would have thought you were in a funeral home judging by all of the sad and unhappy people in Lexington that evening.

I am often embarrassed today to talk about how we acted that evening. I have told many people that if psychiatrists had been watching our behavior during that game, they may have had every one of us committed to an insane asylum. As I look back, it was amazing what an emotional high and low I experienced in just a matter of two minutes, and I was not even a direct participant in this competition. This is one example of what competition can do to you if you are completely invested in an activity.

Now you may ask what this story has to do with the Ladder to Success. It is actually one of the common reasons that people quit trying to climb the ladder. When people experience the pain that comes with losing, many of them will decide not to participate in that activity again. Others will be hesitant and ready to jump off the ladder and quit at the first sign of losing.

In reference to the UK-Duke game, I know of some individuals in my community today that have quit being avid UK fans because they experienced so much hurt that evening. While this is drastic, many people will alter their involvement in competitive activities because of negative experiences and losses. They may eventually get involved again, but they may not invest their hearts into the competition.

The sad reality for those people, however, is that while they will not experience the strong feeling of hurt associated with losing, they will also never experience the true joy associated with victory. When I think of this dilemma, two expressions come to my mind. The first is "hollow victory", while the second is "bandwagon fan."

A hollow victory can occur when people do not invest their hearts into something, but they still achieve victory. Even though they have won the competition, they still do not experience the feelings of euphoria that others enjoy who have invested their hearts into winning. Bandwagon fans are those who wait until a team is winning and highly successful before they choose to become a supporter. In both cases, these people are essentially playing it safe.

While they will not completely experience the agony of defeat, they will also never achieve the levels of excitement and pure joy that people experience after they put their hearts into a victory. Legendary football coach Vince Lombardi summed up this concept best when he said, "I firmly believe that any man's finest hours – his greatest fulfillment of all that he holds dear – is that moment when he has worked his heart out in good cause and lies exhausted on the field of battle – victorious."

Now, while all of this sounds easy enough, how do you go about implementing this approach with the young people in your life? The danger with competitive behavior in young people is that you must achieve a balance of sportsmanship, teamwork, and competitive drive. This is very hard to accomplish with young children. As we are all very aware, toddlers and preschool age children are usually selfish. While there are some exceptions, most young children only see their needs and wants as important. Through repeated instruction from adults and playing with other children, most youngsters eventually become more willing to share and exercise teamwork with others.

However, the more competitive young children become, the less likely they will be willing to share and display teamwork with others. The dilemma becomes that we do not want to stifle competitive drive, but we still need to help our young people develop good sportsmanship and the ability to work with others on a team.

Even though they had not researched the topic, I think my family had the right approach with me as a young child. When I wanted to play a game, whether it was Monopoly or any other competitive game at home, my family often found a way for me to win. I didn't realize what they were doing then, but as I look back, they wanted me to experience success. They always encouraged me to participate in competitive activities, and they usually found a way for me to achieve victory. To this day, I can still remember my grandmother telling me that I could be successful at anything.

Now this was not too hard to accomplish in a controlled environment at home, but when I took part in outside team activities such as Little League baseball, my family no longer had the ability to help me achieve success. As a matter of fact, I experienced the harsh pain of failure when I was cut as a nine-year old trying out for the Pirates Little League team in my community.

Unlike the no-cut rules of today, where everybody makes a team if you try out, I had to go through tryouts which were followed by cuts. The number of available roster spots on each team depended on how many kids the team lost from the year before. It was just my luck that the Pirates only had one available roster spot that year, and an older boy who was very talented had moved to our community from out of state.

I performed very well in the tryouts, but the other boy earned the roster spot and I was cut from the team. The coach told me that I would have been the next one chosen if there had been a second roster spot. Even though that should have made me feel good, it still did not take away the hurt of being cut.

I could have quit my baseball career at that point, but instead, I looked forward to the next season when I just knew I would make the team. Unfortunately, the Pirates' coach did not manage a team the next year, and I was drafted by a different team. I had a terrible tryout that year, and I was cut for the second straight year. That level of discouragement did cause me to not tryout the following two seasons, but my family never stopped encouraging me to participate.

When I was thirteen, I decided to participate in a tryout for Babe Ruth, which was the next level of baseball in my community, and I wound up playing for three years. I enjoyed that experience so much, and it would have never happened if I had decided to never play baseball again.

I truly don't believe I would have had the drive or the confidence to play again if my family had not worked so hard to help me succeed in competitive activities at home. They always worked hard to make me feel good about myself. Now, it was easier to practice in my home as a youngster because I was the only child until I was nine years old. I had no real sibling rivalries, and I had four people in my home who were constantly giving me positive attention.

Now that I am a parent of three, I definitely see the difficulties of pulling off this method with multiple children in the same house. When we play a game in our home, even if it is as simple as Uno, two of my children will have to lose every time. When my children were really young, I would take time to play competitive games with each of them individually. We would still play games as a family, but I would try to balance it with individual competitive activities so each of my children could experience some success.

A good example of balancing success among my children happened several years ago on Easter Sunday. I was hiding Easter eggs for my two youngest. Ally was always very perceptive and good at finding things, while Sawyer was younger and not yet patient when it came to finding Easter eggs. When they started hunting, Ally had found four eggs before Sawyer had discovered any. So, I started helping Sawyer locate some of the eggs. I wanted to make it even, but when we finished, Sawyer had actually found more eggs. Ally was disappointed because I had unfairly helped Sawyer win.

Instead of stopping there, I insisted on hiding the eggs again. This time I did not lend such a helping hand to Sawyer, and Ally would up finding the most eggs during the second hunt. Sawyer started to act disappointed, but I quickly reminded him that he had found the most during the first hunt. This effort may seem like too much work for some people, but I think it is critical to find ways to help every child gain confidence in their abilities.

Now some of you might be thinking this advice goes against the Ladder to Success because we should teach children that failure is a tool to achieve success. However, opportunities like this are important because it is hard for young children to buy into this philosophy if they don't reach that highest rung and achieve success sometimes. While it is definitely good for children to experience some failure, it is not good for them to experience repeated failure in all of their activities without ever achieving success. If we can help youngsters achieve success when we have controlled environments, we will make it easier for them to use failure as a motivating factor to keep trying for success when they are in more difficult competitive activities. We all need to be active "directors" in our kids' lives. We can't sit around waiting for a learning experience. Instead, we need to actually create those experiences as often as we possibly can.

"The Game Within the Game"

Little Mason was a plump kid, with thick glasses and full of boyhood energy, and with an appetite that wouldn't quit. When he asked his mom and dad if he could play soccer, they winced at the thought of those grueling workouts and the quality of play on "game day".

"Can he handle it," his mom asked after supper when Mason had run outside to play.

"He'll never know until he tries." Dad took his little guy to the mall to buy him a soccer ball.

So, when the youth league applications were taken up at school, Mason proudly turned his in, complete with his signed agreement that once he started practice with his team, he would not quit, and would participate faithfully all the way through the season ending tournament, and post season banquet—a total of ten weeks of practice and games.

When the first workout rolled around, Mason couldn't wait for school to be let out that day. His mom picked him up and drove him to the ball field, and when he was given his uniform at the end of practice, he ran to the car with a huge smile on his face.

"I'm a soccer player, Mom!"

"You are indeed, little man!" And Mason talked non-stop all the way home, explaining every thing his coach had gone over, and every detail of every drill.

After a couple of weeks, game one rolled around. Mason had realized that he was not in very good shape, and in scrimmages he seemed to be awkwardly behind the other players—not only in speed and agility but also in the basics of the game.

Mason's dad met his mom after work and they anxiously sat in the bleachers as the opposing team took the field for warm-ups, and seemed to be awfully good. "I doubt he'll get into this game, Honey." Dad was trying to be realistic, and did not want Mom disappointed.

But about halfway through the second half, with the other team way ahead, Mason's coach told him to go in and play backfield, right in front of the goalie. A couple of times he got his foot on the ball only to have it stolen away, and once he and a teammate collided…but for his first time, he did pretty good. His dad breathed a sigh of relief as the horn sounded, and the game was over.

"Son, proud of you! Let's go get a milkshake to celebrate your first game as a soccer player."

"No, I want to go home! The coach said he wants all of us going to the burger place down the street to have a meal as a team, and I'm not going. We got stomped, I played awful, and I don't feel like having a team meal tonight."

"Honey, why do you say that? I thought you played very well." Mason's mom tried to cheer him up and was hurt that he had such negative emotions after his first game.

"Nope, we don't treat the coach that way, Son." Dad's voice was assertive—even a bit irritated. "If Coach says the team is to meet after the game, there is no decision to be made. We'll go have a snack at the burger shop."

"But Dad, I don't even want to play anymore. I'm no good at soccer!" Mason threw his head in his hands and sobbed. His parents were silent as his dad drove to the team gathering.

Game two came too soon, as Mason had struggled in practices to hold his own. When he was put in the game late in the first half, he took a blunt lick from an opposing player and went down with a badly bruised shin.

"Now can I quit?", he asked his dad as he came to the car after the game with an ice wrap on his leg.

"What do you mean, Son? You played your best, you got hit pretty hard...but your leg should be fine by next week. Did the coach suggest you should hang it up for this year?"

"No—I only wish...Dad, I hate soccer. I can't play. I'm no good!"

"Mason, Son, do you know Bradley Snedegar?"

"Of course—he's in my homeroom at school."

"Did you know that Bradley bowls in a weekend league even though he's confined to a wheelchair?"

"Yea, he told me something about that."

"Do you think if Bradley can dig down deep and do something extra special despite his handicap, that there's a lesson in there somewhere for all of us?"

"But Dad!"

Mason kept plugging along and started noticing that he was losing some weight, and in better shape than he'd ever been. And in practice, Coach used him some as a backup goalie—which he loved, although it made him nervous. But he realized that he could really punt the ball pretty far, and he had steady, soft hands, or at least that's what his coach kept reminding him.

Finally, the last game of the season came. Mason's mom and dad sat in the bleachers before the game and reminisced about how much they had enjoyed their son's first year playing on a ball team. They had made friends with other parents, they had learned a lot about soccer, and they had watched Mason learn some invaluable lessons about life, and not quitting.

But, as they relaxed and chatted, noticing that the score was tied and typically in these close contests Mason did not play late in the game, their team's goalie went down after a scramble for the ball in front of his goal line. Surprisingly, he did not get up. Time was called, a doctor in the crowd was summoned to the field, and the boy was carried off with an apparent broken leg.

"Mason, you're in. You know what to do."

As Coach called out his name, Mason's parents held hands tight, and for what seemed like an eternity, they watched their son stand tall in the arena—scooping up kick after kick from the opposing team, punting out long high balls that kept his team out of danger, and squinting through his glasses on every play as if to say, "I know what I'm doing—I'm a soccer player!"

In the last minute, the opposing team scored two quick goals, and Mason's team lost, 3-1. But after the game, he did not come off the field crying, or complaining. He just came over and hugged his Mom and Dad and said, "Coach wants us to meet for pizza after the game. So, let's go."

Little Mason hung up his cleats after that game…Not because he didn't like soccer, but as he grew–other, faster and more experienced kids were playing soccer in the youth league and at his school. He realized that over the long haul, he needed to find hobbies that he was more suited for. But, later on, in high school, he did hook back up with the game—as a trainer. The high school coach loved his work ethic, his knowledge of the game, and how he was almost like an extra coach with the players.

And when Mason went to college, he played intramural soccer for a couple of years, and loved it. Later, as an adult, he volunteered as a coach in his hometown's YMCA league.

And on his mantle at work, where he now oversees a team of twenty-five employees and is known as one of the smartest, kindest, most effective leaders in the organization, sits the team picture of that first youth soccer team. On the front row, kneeling down, with his glasses on and holding a soccer ball in his hands, is little Mason.

When asked why that picture holds such prominence, Mason simply says, "Because that fall, Mom and Dad, and Coach, and my teammates…they helped me learn what it takes to succeed in life. I learned more by having to sit the bench and hang in there for the team—even though there was not much reason for me personally to do so—than anything else I have done in my entire life. That was the year I started "getting it". I cherish the "climb up the hill" I had to struggle through that fall. You see, the "climb" is in reality the 'game of life'.

Questions for Reflection

1. What is your school's philosophy on balancing competitive and cooperative experiences for students?
2. Have the children in your life developed any bad habits in recreational venues (inside or outside of school) in their approach to participating in competitive activities?
3. What training is your school or community providing in how to be productive students and athletes who have a healthy understanding of competition?
4. Is there training also provided to parents?
5. Have you ever designed any competitive activities to help your children or students achieve success?

In Outliers, *Malcolm Gladwell (2008) explores the unique habits of successful people. The extraordinary "breaks" that seem to fall in the lap of some individuals are in reality often the results of a competitive spirit of consistent hard work, over a period of several years, that takes them to a higher level.*

Two P's in a Pod – Perseverance and Perfection
Step 8

The words perseverance and perfection are not usually grouped together, but I have found through my experience that there is an important relationship between these words which can help shape young people into successful adults and leaders.

I think everyone would agree that perseverance is an important quality in all successful leaders. As a matter of fact, perseverance is the factor that allows each of us to push on up the ladder when we reach failure. Without this trait, Edison would definitely have not kept working after failing so many times trying to invent the light bulb. Perseverance is what helped George Washington lead America to gain independence in the Revolutionary War. As a matter of fact, history is full of cases where perseverance helped groups of ordinary people achieve extraordinary results.

I like to think of perseverance as the ability to stay on course or keep pushing forward when faced with struggles or obstacles. In the cases I mentioned above, it would have been easy to quit or change course when Edison or Washington encountered failure or disappointment. Instead, they pushed ahead even stronger and more determined to achieve success.

When trying to break down the components of perseverance, competitive drive is one obvious ingredient. Another component which was discussed back in Step 4 is self-discipline. In terms of leadership development, self-discipline is the ability to develop routines and maintain a high level of diligence and persistence in pursuing goals. Unfortunately, self-discipline is often the hardest leadership trait to learn as a young person. The reason for this is that self-discipline is a daily process, and not an occasional event. Also, it is often in direct conflict with current desires and impulses.

A good example of the difficulty in trying to develop self-discipline is someone trying to get into better physical shape and improve eating habits. How many of you have made New Year's resolutions to begin working out and improve your health only to see your efforts fade away within a couple of months? The reason for this is that working out and eating better requires a consistent daily effort. Positive habits have to be developed, and this may require getting up earlier than we wish or turning down a dessert after a meal that we are craving. Unfortunately most people cannot maintain that level of self-discipline and dedication and will skip following the necessary routine on some days. Then, when they don't see the results they desire, they just eventually quit altogether.

Perseverance is also related to the earlier chapter topics of motivation and responsibility. Both intrinsic and fear-based motivation can lead one to develop greater levels of perseverance and self-discipline. One may have a strong enough desire to develop the habits and drive necessary to keep moving forward even when times become difficult. Also, one may face a serious life event such as a heart attack which causes enough fear to develop high levels of self-discipline and perseverance to make healthy decisions.

Responsibility is another key factor as people with high levels of responsibility tend to have greater levels of perseverance. Their sense of responsibility sparks a desire to push ahead even when obstacles get in the way of achieving a goal. Overall, the combination of competitive drive, self-discipline, motivation, and responsibility create the formula for perseverance that can make a huge difference in achieving success.

Perfection, on the other hand, is something that is often talked about and sought after by many people, but it is more of a mysterious topic. Some scholars even say that complete perfection is impossible to achieve. Other people classify many things in life as perfect. The reason for the differences of opinion is that perfection is held in the eyes of the beholder.

In other words, what may be perfect to one person can be awful to another. A good example of this is any of the musical talent shows that have flooded television in recent years, such as American Idol. How many times have you felt like a performance was absolutely perfect only to hear one of the judges be extremely critical? This is just one example of how perfection is entirely based on individual viewpoints.

One reason that perfection is so hard to gauge is because it entirely depends on our own individual expectations and what we define as perfect in each event we encounter in life. For people who have extremely high expectations for an activity or an event, perfection is very difficult to achieve. However, if someone has relatively low expectations, he or she might more easily deem an event to be perfect. It could even be the same event where another person is disappointed with the outcome.

For instance, a day at the beach might be absolutely perfect to someone who is on a vacation and is thrilled to get away from the daily grind of work. However, that same beautiful day at the beach might be disappointing to someone who frequents the beach often and is coming there to surf only to find that the waves are down a little that afternoon.

Another factor that can impact our view of perfection is our own level of interest and passion surrounding an activity. If we partake in an activity that we completely enjoy, then we create an opportunity for that event to be perfect in our eyes. It does not mean that every time we participate in that activity we will deem it to be perfect, but it does mean that the potential for perfection exists. On the other hand, if we strongly dislike an activity, it is impossible for us to consider the event to be perfect.

I will give you a couple of personal examples to illustrate this point. I really enjoy being outside and I love to go to a nearby state park to hike on the nature trails. My wife Stacy, on the other hand, does not enjoy being outside, and she despises walking on trails. A few years ago, I finally talked her into going to this state park, and we walked on one of the trails. To me, this was a perfect afternoon, but to her, it was misery.

Even though Stacy does not enjoy walking on nature trails, she can happily walk miles around a mall shopping for new clothes. We can spend a day at the mall, and she can find that day to be perfect while I find little enjoyment shopping for women's clothes. At the end of both activities, we may have walked the same distance, but our opinions about which event could be perfect are totally opposite.

Yet, the most significant variable that can impact our pursuit of perfection is attitude. Of all the factors that can affect whether we deem something to be perfect, attitude is the most important. Having a positive attitude is critical if we are to ever experience perfection. If we allow ourselves to develop a negative attitude, it is impossible for anything in our lives to be perfect.

When I think of this topic, the image of Debbie Downer always pops into my head. Debbie Downer was an NBC Saturday Night Live character played by Rachel Dratch. Debbie is someone who always has a negative attitude about everything. No matter how positive a situation may seem, Debbie can always ruin the moment. She always sees the worst in everything and as a result, she is never happy. In the SNL skits, people around Debbie usually experience something positive, but Debbie will quickly come back with something negative to bring down the people around her. If you think about it, a negative attitude is like poison because it kills anything it touches. Not only can you ruin your own experiences, but you can also prevent those around you from feeling joy or perfection. Instead, a positive attitude will make your experiences better, and it can also lift the spirits of everyone around you.

Now that we have cleared up some of the confusion surrounding the topic of perfection, let's look at the term perfectionist. A perfectionist is someone who insists on making every detail of his or her life perfect. Like most things, there are varying degrees of perfectionism. Some people are just very particular and want things in their lives to be handled a certain way.

Other people, however, can be so severely focused on perfection that they exhibit behavior associated with OCD (obsessive-compulsive disorder). Perfectionists can display obsessive or compulsive behavior which can be very destructive. Thomas Greenspon has published professional articles and written books dealing with the topic of perfectionism, and he identifies a distinction between perfectionists and high achievers. He has indicated that perfectionist characteristics can be detrimental to young people. However, other research indicates that healthy doses of perfectionism can exist. Don Hamachek has identified two types of perfectionism – normal and neurotic. Healthy perfectionists have strivings for excellence but lower concerns about mistakes, while unhealthy perfectionists have strivings for excellence coupled with high levels of concerns about failure. I completely agree with this body of research, as the key factor to having healthy levels of perfectionism is maintaining a positive outlook on failure.

Once again, the Ladder to Success can help young people maintain strivings for excellence while understanding that failure is only one step away from success. From my experience in education, children who have relatively non-existent levels of healthy perfectionism tend to be less successful. They may have an easy going personality and may be well liked by those around them, but success for these individuals is generally inconsistent.

With that said, I have also witnessed several children on the opposite end of the spectrum who seemed to always be nervous wrecks. These children tend to be preoccupied with perfectionism, but they are petrified by the thought of failure. Unfortunately, for some of these children, their parents have made them feel like failures if they do not achieve constant success. This type of pressure can mount on children and cause them to be unhealthy perfectionists.

I want to make a point that unhealthy perfectionism is not always a result of parental pressure. Some children naturally put too much pressure on themselves. I can relate to this because I most definitely suffered from this tendency at times during my childhood. My family never scolded me for not achieving success, but instead, I seemed to scold myself. I placed tremendous pressure on myself to be perfect in everything I did as a child.

Unfortunately, many of my actions became compulsive as I demonstrated many characteristics of OCD behavior. I tried to cover up this bad habit around my friends and family, but at times, it would drive me crazy. Fortunately, one of the greatest positives for me during my childhood was that I was highly successful. I was always at or near the top of my class in school. Another positive was that my family was always extremely supportive of me and did not pressure or scold me. If I would have had pressure from them, I might have gone over the edge.

I can remember how I used to make sure that everything was exactly perfect or I would get extremely upset with myself. I remember feeling like things would go wrong if I didn't do everything in an exact order. A lot of my behavior seemed superstitious, as I did not want to step on cracks in the sidewalk, and I had to enter rooms with my left foot. I also used to study for hours to make sure that every word of my homework was perfect.

I continued this behavior until my sophomore year of high school, when I finally made an internal decision to stop worrying about making every detail of my homework perfect. I decided to still shoot for an "A" in every class, but I no longer demanded complete perfection of myself. It took some time, but this resulted in much less self-imposed stress and pressure. I made my first and only "B's" of my high school career during that year of my life, which did disappoint me a great deal.

After a while, I was able to balance things better. I developed great confidence in my abilities to study for exams in a short period of time. I learned that I could still achieve great results without spending enormous energy laboring over every detail of an activity.

I still wanted to achieve perfection, but I no longer was beating myself up when I did not always achieve it. This slowly helped me to drop some of my other compulsive behavior tendencies. The most pleasing result for me was that with this new outlook, I still achieved success as I made straight "A's" over my last two years of high school without feeling immense stress.

My advice for parents, teachers, administrators and coaches is to encourage young people in their lives to strive for a healthy level of perfectionism in everything they do, but understand that mistakes and failure will occur on the road to achievement. Navigating that line between healthy and unhealthy perfectionism is an enormous challenge, but one that is critical to helping young people achieve sustained success.

"...perseverance and perfection can work together to help young people achieve at high levels."

By incorporating the principles of the Ladder to Success, you can always encourage children to achieve their very best while helping them to understand that when they fail, success is just around the corner as long as they have perseverance. This is where the two "P's" in a pod come into play, as perseverance and perfection can work together to help young people achieve at high levels.

And as a word of caution, it is important to remember that perseverance combined with mediocrity will not produce outstanding results. Many people in this world push onward and persevere through enormously difficult circumstances, but they strive for nothing better and are satisfied living in their same environment. Therefore, their circumstances never change, even though they fight to survive and keep going.

However, those people who strive for perfection and don't let mistakes or failures bring them down will generally persevere and achieve success. We must foster an atmosphere where children can combine healthy perfectionism and perseverance to achieve success, while understanding that failures will often occur as they climb up the ladder. As adults who are significant in the lives of children, it is our responsibility to help young people develop this very important point of view.

"I Can Do It All"

Alice was out the door as soon as her supper was over. She had gulped it down before her family even had time to sit and enjoy a meal together.

"Alice, where are you going?" Her mom was visibly upset. "You do this every night it seems, Honey. Can't you even take time to eat?"

"We've got a show tomorrow, Mom. We'll be at the field practicing until after dark."

Alice was in her high school's marching band, and she was part of the drum core. Fall marching season had begun, and the hours of practice in preparation for football games and competitions seemed a bit extreme to Alice's parents, but they did not want her to not live up to the expectations of her band director.

On Sunday afternoon, Alice forfeited her ritual of taking a long nap after church and headed for the library.

"Now where are you going, Honey?" Her mom felt so helpless.

"Academic team cram session—we have a huge meet tomorrow evening."

Monday, after school, Alice accepted an invitation by the girls' basketball coach to begin pre-season workouts with the team. She had played back in middle school, and her friends had said for a long time that she was one of the best athletes in her class. So, she wanted to give it a try. And, she signed up to teach a dance class at the elementary school later on in the winter.

"Alice….how will you keep up?" Her mom yelled in frustration this time when Alice came home and shared the news.

"I thought you'd be happy, Mom. You and Dad used to love to come watch me play when I was a little kid. Why are you on me all the time these days?"

Her mom's voice broke, as she sat down on the sofa and began to cry.

"Alice, all we ever wanted was for you to be happy, and do your best. Your older brother played ball in college, and is now in med school, because he always did his best. But Honey, you seem obsessed with achievement. You seem obsessed with staying so busy you can't even slow down to eat and sleep. You won't be able to keep this pace for long, Alice. It will catch up with you."

"Mom, what about Neil? He's so spoiled he can't even put his coat on by himself and he does nothing but play and do what he wants all day. He's going to be the first in this family to flunk out of grade school!"

"Neil is three years old. Plus, he probably sees your frantic pace and has decided he wants no part of it. Stop avoiding the issue Alice."

"And what about Dad? He works long hours during the week, volunteers down town most Saturdays, then back to work on Monday."

"Your Dad is doing what he feels led to do — making sure he can pay for your and your older brother's college education. Plus, he does eat healthy, he does exercise, and he does get plenty of sleep. He is fulfilled–he loves his job and his volunteer projects. And, he makes time for his hobbies. Your father lives a very well balanced life. You could learn a thing or two from him. "

"I have hobbies."

"Honey, lately, all of your hobbies seem to turn into obsessions, with you feeling like you have to prove you're perfect. You don't have to prove that to anyone."

"And you, Mom? You're down at the bank all day, plus president of the women's club, playing tennis at the Y a lot, running us kids here and there, involved at church."

"Actually, Alice, I love my life. When I do over-book my calendar, I have learned to cut back. I work hard to maintain a good balance—my faith, my family, my work, my hobbies…in that order. But, it's taken me years to learn what works for me, and I'm just trying to warn you, I can tell—you're over-doing it…You're so much like me when I was your age."

Alice was surprised to hear her mom say this, and sat down at the kitchen table. "You were like me?"

"Sure was, Honey. And I remember how those days were…it was hard to say 'no' when so many exciting opportunities presented themselves. Please don't misunderstand–your father and I are so, so proud of you for how you excel in everything you do. All we're concerned about is, you must not push yourself over the brink thinking it does not have a negative impact on your mind, body, and spirit after a while. Because, always, it does."

"But Mom, I can handle it. There are a lot of people depending on me."

"Really? And how would they feel if someday you weren't there at all for them?"

"How do you mean?"

"Alice, I had a great friend in high school–her name was Marci. And, well, Marci was the brightest, most talented kid in our class. She could do anything, and as a result, people asked her to do everything. She was on the track team, she was in Beta Club, she was the editor of our school paper, she was a cheerleader, she was a volunteer with the scouts, and she was on the golf team. She even worked in the front office during her study hall."

"Sounds like she had it together pretty well to me."

"Oh, that's what we all thought, Alice. Then one day, Marci didn't come to school, and her parents had no clue where she was. Later that morning, the police found her car over an embankment. She was in it, lifeless, and had apparently fallen asleep at the wheel on her way to school. Her parents were heart broken, and when they started investigating her schedule more closely over the past year, they realized that she had been pushing herself to the point of only getting a few hours of sleep at night, not eating right, running here and there and everywhere to keep up, and not having time for her family and friends. She had let her life get out of control."

"What could she have done different, Mom? She loved all those things she was doing. That was her life."

"Exactly. That was her life, and she was doing it all as if she had no tomorrow. Thus, she worked herself day and night in an OCD world she allowed to entrap her, that finally led to an accident that indeed did not give her a tomorrow. But Alice, my precious Alice, there was a better way."

"But how? I'll admit, Marci sounds a lot like me."

"Balance. If Marci had only understood the critical importance of balance, she would have most likely lived one of the most fulfilling, successful, impacting lives this county has ever known."

"But with all that important stuff she was excelling at, I'd say she was extremely balanced, Mom."

"Not if she was not leaving time for her health, her family, her peace of mind. She understood how to be persistent at striving to be perfect. But she never understood that there is a balance factor. And when a person, any person, loses touch with that 'center', then their life will begin to spin out of control."

"So you think I'm unbalanced, Mom?"

"No, I think you've excelled so much in your young life that you get your energy, your self-esteem, by pleasing other people who you feel must see you doing something to perfection. It can happen to all of us. It's not a bad thing when it's within reason. Actually, it's quite noble. But, it's harmful over the long haul if not mastered in moderation. I love you dearly, Alice. I want you to keep being such a blessing to those around you…for a lifetime. I want you to keep striving for perfection. I want you to keep being persistent in using and developing your array of talents. But, I also want you to slow down and spread them out in a way that's reasonable."

"So, perhaps I should not play basketball right now. Maybe later on, and perhaps I should schedule in some down time every day — like for meals, some time just to think and relax, and for a good night's sleep. And perhaps I should spend more time on Saturdays playing tennis with you. I used to love that when I was little."

"I think those are great ideas."

"I love you Mom. Thank you — I needed this talk more than you know."

Questions for Reflection

1. Do you know of students who struggle with the 'super kid' syndrome, involved in so many activities they have little time for a normal life?

2. Does your school foster a culture of "spreading the wealth around" — encouraging the entire student population to share the responsibilities?

3. Do you yourself struggle with OCD tendencies in regard to work?

4. What are areas of your life that need fine tuning if you are to find that magical balance of perseverance and perfection that leads to fulfillment and completeness?

5. Does your school or organization create a frenzied OCD work culture of endless tasks?

In Leadership and Self Deception *(The Arbinger Institute, 2000), the reader takes a look inside, as the blind spots that we all tend to overlook about ourselves are exposed.*

Unlocking the Potential in a Difficult Child
Step 9

Of all the chapters in this book, this is by far the one I have dreaded to write the most. It is not because I don't have any experience with this topic or because it is less important than the other chapters. The reason I have been so hesitant is that I have been very humbled by this topic over the course of my life, and I have changed my point of view in many ways when it comes to dealing with a difficult child. For many of you, this may be one of the most important chapters in the book. For others, it may not even be an issue.

As you know by now, I am the father of three children, and until my third child was born, I did not really understand the dynamics of an obstinate child. I used to be the parent who walked through the grocery store and shook my head in disbelief as other parents would struggle with out of control children. I would scoff at the frustration and anger they directed toward their kids. I could not believe that any good parent would allow their children to misbehave in public in this manner.

I am sure you have heard of people having to eat their words. Well, let's just say I could have a feast on the number of times I have eaten my words after Stacy and I had our third child, Sawyer. With our first two children, everything was relatively easy even though at the time I didn't always see it that way. The behavior issues we faced with Reiley and Ally as children pale in comparison to the problems we encountered with Sawyer as a young child. Both Reiley and Ally listened when Stacy and I communicated clear behavior expectations.

Now, I don't want to paint a perfectly rosy picture. Reiley and Ally were not always perfect angels, but they were generally always on their best behavior both at school and in public. If we were in a store, and I asked either one of them to stop doing something, they stopped doing it. I thought this was a result of my good parenting and clear behavior expectations. I also assumed that all of those unruly children I experienced in public behaved this way as a result of poor parenting.

Oh was I ever fooled! From the time Sawyer started walking, it was apparent he had an iron will to do exactly whatever he wanted to do regardless of whether we approved or not. As a small child, Sawyer was demanding of every ounce of our attention. If we were in public, he would not stay in a cart. If he wanted something, he would throw a fit when we didn't get it for him. With our other children, we could scold their inappropriate behavior and explain to them how we expected them to behave. They may not have been happy, but they always listened. Often, I could even give a stern look if they started misbehaving in public, and they would instantly change their behavior.

However, Sawyer was a completely different story as a young child. Stern looks did not even put a dent in his actions. Having a talk with him about his behavior usually got little response. At home, timeouts had some limited effectiveness at best. I know many experts are against spanking, but at times, some of Sawyer's actions were so severe that spanking seemed necessary. Once again, this had limited effectiveness. If there is a form of disciplining your child, we probably tried it at one time or another.

Now, before I go any further, I want to clarify some things about Sawyer. By now, many of you probably think that he was a terrible child, but that is definitely not the case. Even though he was extremely difficult to deal with at times, Sawyer is one of the kindest and most loving children in the world. As a young child, he hugged nearly everyone he met, and he was always the first to help others when they needed assistance.

However, when something would upset Sawyer, all of that sweet kindness disappeared, and he became consumed with anger. When he reached this point, there was nothing you could do to change his temperament, and he had no ability to use reason or logic. We would have to grab him by the hand, and physically leave the situation, but this rarely happened without causing a scene. This was a regular occurrence when Sawyer was a toddler and even at preschool age. As he has grown up, he has overcome these behavior issues but he still has a very strong willed personality.

Before examining strategies for helping children with behavior issues reach their full potential, we need to dispel a primary myth surrounding this topic. First of all, anyone who claims that children are a complete product of their environment has never had more than one child. The reason I wanted to explain my personal parenting situation was to allow all of those troubled mothers and fathers out there to stop beating themselves up over their apparent inability to be great parents.

I can assure you that a large part of a child's personality and behavior are related to genetics. If you talk to people who have three or more children, they will definitely back up this theory. It does not mean that one of their children is necessarily a problem child, but they can all point to distinct differences in their children even though they have provided the same living environment. My oldest child Reiley shares some distinct personality traits that I had as a young child. I was always very outgoing until it came to having a girlfriend. I was always very shy and afraid of rejection when it came to approaching girls. I have always remembered that uneasy feeling, and I worked very hard to encourage Reiley not to have those feelings.

However, those attempts were futile as Reiley was possibly even worse as a young child than me. When he was in preschool, if we even mentioned a girl around him, he would get very upset and run to his room out of embarrassment. I often remarked to Stacy how much he reminded me of my own behavior at that age even though I had never discussed or encouraged that behavior with him.

Sawyer, on the other hand, was a ladies' man as a young child. When he was just six, he began talking to a girl who played in his soccer league. One day after a game, we were getting ready to leave when Sawyer asked me to hold on a minute. He ran back toward the field and began talking to the girl again. After a few seconds, he ran back to me and said that he had asked her to be his girlfriend. He immediately began trying to plan out a date to the movies with her. Now isn't that a vast difference among siblings even though as parents we did nothing any different to encourage such opposite behaviors?

Stacy and I had the fortune of having two children first who behaved quite well. In one respect, this gave us the confidence to better deal with the issues surrounding a strong willed child. We are just very happy that we had our children in the order we did. However, this brings up another point that could have an effect on child misbehavior – birth order. Even though I think that a lot of Sawyer's obstinate behavior is genetic, the issue of birth order still needs to be addressed. There is no doubt that a lot of the behavior issues we encountered with Sawyer were related to disputes or problems with Reiley or Ally. I also recognize as a parent that I was much more patient and full of energy with Reiley and Ally.

With Sawyer, my patience was thin, and I often felt worn out. I sometimes gave in or just gave up, when I know I would have made a larger effort as a young parent of one child in dealing with issues in the right manner. I know that some of this is probably related to age and stress, as over 20 years of being a parent can take a toll on someone. Also, the divided attention that is required to be a good parent to three children also has a big effect on the amount of quality time I could spend individually with each child.

While Sawyer did not share some of the traits that Reiley and I seemed to share genetically, much of his obstinate behavior reminded me of stories I had heard from my family about my early childhood. I was very strong willed, but unlike Sawyer's situation, I was the only child in a home of four caregivers during the first nine years of my life. That extra attention helped me a great deal, but I was not able to provide that level of attention to Sawyer with only two caregivers and three children in our home.

In addition to the problems that multiple children and age can pose for parents, birth order presents a variety of potential issues for children whether they are the oldest, youngest, or somewhere in between. For instance, Sawyer has always felt like he should be able to do everything that Reiley does, even though Reiley is seven years older. Also, as Reiley and Ally began inviting friends over more often, Sawyer would feel left out because he was excluded from many of the activities they planned with their friends.

As the oldest, Reiley has always felt like we were harder on him, and he constantly felt like we allowed Ally and Sawyer to do things he would not have been allowed to do at that age. Ally has often felt like she was left out of things as the only girl, but at least she has never seemed to experience the "middle child syndrome." Actually, as the only girl, she has gotten a lot of special attention that is unique. I think that if she had been a boy, things could have been much worse as the middle child of three.

I think I have given enough background information about our children, but it is very important to understand that children with behavior issues are not necessarily a direct result of poor parenting. With that said, I also don't think it is fair to attribute all negative child behavior issues to genetics or birth order. As a former high school principal, I have definitely observed my fair share of discipline problems, and there have been many times that immediately following a parent conference, I could see that the child was a carbon copy of the behavior modeled by the parent. Actually, my experiences have led me to understand three vastly different parenting styles that often result in child behavior problems.

The first and most recognizable parenting style that can lead to child behavior problems is what I call the controlling and aggressive style. This type of parent is demanding and often demeaning to their children, sometimes bordering on being verbally abusive. In milder cases, the parent may rather appear stern and overbearing toward their children.

The resulting behavior for the child is generally one of two extremes. Many of these children mimic their parents and are aggressive toward others. They tend to exhibit bullying behavior and often get in verbal disputes or physical fights with other children. Some children, however, will completely withdraw. They may either be submissive or just quiet with hidden feelings of anger and frustration. Neither of these resulting behaviors can be identified as positive. The first type of child usually stays in trouble at school, while the second type usually lags behind. However, the pent up frustration can sometimes lead to dangerous or self-destructive behavior because of such low levels of self-esteem.

The second type of parenting style that leads to behavior problems is what I call the absent parenting syndrome. In this case, the parent is often self-absorbed and makes little time for their children. This same style can actually describe two different types of parents. Some parents that fit this style are actually quite successful people who provide material items for their children, but they are too busy to ever spend much quality time with their family. We often identify these people as good parents from distant observations because they work to provide many things for their children, but we don't see their lack of a close personal family relationship. The other type of parent usually has personal problems and may be a single parent, or could possibly have a drug or alcohol problem. This parent usually has little or no role in their children's lives.

The end result for children from both types of parents can once again go to either extreme. They may be quite wild in their behavior because they do not feel any accountability to a parent. They may seek to find companionship with the wrong group of people so they can get the attention they are craving. On the other hand, some children with absent parents actually become quite independent.

However, with little or no guidance, they can often be defensive and even display a lack of moral character.

The final type of parenting that can lead to behavior problems is the smothering and spoiling parenting style. Unfortunately, this parenting style is becoming very common today. The bad thing is that parents like this are often viewed from the outside as good parents because they are so involved in the lives of their children. And the truth of the matter is that they are indeed good parents in many respects.

Children from these homes usually have nice clothes and they never go without the food they want to eat. These parents generally sit down with their children and make sure their homework is complete for school each day, and they nearly always attend parent-teacher conferences while their children are in elementary school.

I think the primary motivating factor for this type of parent is that they strive to make sure their children have smooth lives and never face any of the difficulties and stumbling blocks they faced as children. The problem for these parents is that they are so concerned with making sure that their children never fail, they completely miss the point that those failures help us build perseverance and the desire to achieve. We have touched on this way of thinking in many chapters and it relates heavily once again with the Ladder to Success.

Even though these strategies that help our children become successful may make perfect sense now, I completely understand how difficult it is to stand back and watch your children fail at something. I have been equally guilty of displaying characteristics of this parenting style even though I know the possible dangers. As a matter of fact, I would venture to guess that most parents reading this book today have displayed some characteristics of this style at some time with their children. I have to work extra hard at making myself step back and not get too involved at times.

Now as a parent, if you read through these negative parenting styles and don't feel that any of the three styles describe you, it is very possible that you may have a few traits of different parenting styles. And while it is possible that you maintain the perfect approach to parenting, there is a good chance that if you look deep enough, you will find that you display a few traits that I have described in one of the three parenting styles. For me, this has been a very humbling experience as I take a hard look at my own parenting. This can be especially difficult if you have some traits like I share with the smothering parenting style. This is difficult because in one respect, you feel like you are just being a loving and caring parent, but it is easy to not see the damage this can be causing to your children.

As we have discussed earlier, teaching responsibility and following the Ladder to Success is important at all stages of a child's growth and development. If parents or significant others step in and complete activities to ensure young children are successful, those children can quickly develop a learned helplessness. They never appropriately develop the ability to solve problems, and achieving success does not bring the high levels of satisfaction and gratification that others enjoy.

To put it simply, these children often take life for granted and have little appreciation for anything. In the field of education, we are just as guilty of promoting this behavior, as high stakes testing pressures teachers and administrators to spoon feed children the information they need to succeed on state and federal mandated tests. In essence, many educators feel almost forced to teach the test. Athletic coaches feel the same pressures as they are expected to win, and they are often encouraged to coddle student athletes who have behavior issues because of demands from parents and others in local communities.

You may ask what significance this discussion on negative parenting styles may have on helping deal with obstinate children, but I think it is important to deeply understand our own parenting styles so we can make necessary adjustments to help our children succeed. Regardless of whether a negative parenting style exists or if you may be a teacher, coach, or significant other, it is vital that we focus on helping children overcome behavior issues. The key to making anything positive happen is to maintain a high level of patience.

As I discussed earlier, this is often easier said than done. However, I think everyone would agree that when you lose your cool, it is hard to help a child make a positive behavior change.

Losing your temper might precipitate a short-term behavior change because of fear on the child's part, but in the long run, it will only reinforce that becoming angry is an acceptable response. On the other extreme, constantly giving in or overlooking misbehavior is not going to help children develop into successful adults either.

The only way to make a positive difference in the long run is to set clear behavior expectations and follow up with consistent responses. When I think of this application in a classroom setting, I always think of an outstanding teacher named Shirley Chafin who I had the pleasure of working with for several years. She had a teaching career that spanned nearly 50 years, and in that time, I never heard of her completely losing her cool or even hardly raising her voice. However, she rarely ever had a discipline problem. She was stern but respected her students, and she was very precise in her expectations.

Many students feared taking her class because she was thought of as a very difficult teacher. On the other hand, those students who finished one of her courses were usually in line to request having her as a teacher again because they had such a wonderful experience.

For parents, setting high behavior expectations that are very clear is crucial to helping children succeed who have behavior problems. As I have noted earlier, when you are dealing with a difficult child, this may not always show immediate results, but you will see improvements over a longer period of time. This is where patience is so important, and unfortunately, sometimes where I still struggle today. As I said at the beginning of the chapter, this has been a very challenging segment to write because I see so many of my own problems as a parent when I reflect on this topic.

On the other hand, I think it is nice for others to feel like they are not failures as parents, teachers, or significant others because they struggle with a strong willed child. I do think that being aware of the issues surrounding this topic can help in making a positive difference in the lives of children with behavior problems.

According to an article by Linda Rodgers on Parenting.com, research conducted by Dr. Christy Buchanan and published in the Journal of Research on Adolescence found that setting high expectations for children is very important because those expectations can become self-fulfilling prophecies. In other words, if we expect our children to behave badly or make poor decisions, we often get what we expect. On the other hand, if children know we have high expectations for them, they generally do not want to let us down.

Rodgers points out that studies on teens and drinking reveal the dangers of parenting to either extreme. It was found that children of permissive parents were three times more likely to drink heavily, while children of overly strict parents faced twice the risk of drinking heavily. Children who had warm relationships with their parents showed the least risk.

It is easy to see that if we are too loose in our expectations, problems can arise. However, having high expectations does not mean that we should be overly strict on children. First, this does not allow them to develop a sense of responsibility. They also feel no sense of trust and often want to rebel when they have a chance to be away from their authority figures.

This research makes it evident that we need to strike the right balance of setting high expectations without trying to control every aspect of a child's life. Ultimately, children know if we care. If we develop positive relationships built on trust and developing responsibility, we will be able to help the children in our lives achieve success.

The worst thing we can do is criticize, or allow our children to think we don't have confidence in their abilities. With Sawyer, I constantly compliment him on all of the great things he does. I have always placed a great focus on his many talents and gifts. By developing a positive self-image, he has been able to mature and achieve at very high levels. He is an extremely gifted person in many areas, and he has grown to understand and appreciate his talents. Even though this is a slower process for both parents and educators, it is the best way to ensure that a child can maintain confidence and grow up to be a high achiever.

"Two Unique Children, and Neither Can Be Me"

"Out tonight with the guys, Dad. Be home in a few."

And off Drew drove, in the family car. Little did his parents know that as a seventeen year old, he was already into regular weekend drinking. And little did they know, but they had led him right to the poison water, from the time he was five years old and on his first ball team.

His younger sis, Allison, knew he drank. She had heard the talk around school, and smelled it on his breath several times recently. But strangely, Mom and Dad didn't have a clue. They were too busy making sure Drew was the perfect kid, on his way to college and a successful life. But they had left out one key part of raising Drew…they had loved being the proud parents of a high achieving kid, yet they had forgotten to love him first as a precious boy, and their only son.

Drew drank to set himself free of the endless pressure. His dad had played high school sports, and excelled. His mom had been a cheerleader in high school and also college. For as long as Drew could remember, his life was about pleasing his folks on the field. They would cancel family vacations, summer camp, even going to church on Sundays if Drew had a game. And, they pressured him to perform at his best, and sometimes above his best, as if he was to earn a college scholarship at one of the best schools in the country. By middle school, Drew hated coming home after a game, because there was always the re-living of every play, and the analyzing of what he could have done differently.

Allison soon hated to go to Drew's ball games as well. No matter how well he did, Mom and Dad seemed to find something to be anxious about...the coaches, the other team's attitude, or Drew's teammates' attitudes. It was as if they were literally obsessed with Drew's ball teams. When Allison's health teacher covered a unit on mental and emotional illness, and explained what OCD was, Allison nodded her head, and wrote down on a piece of paper to herself, "Mom and Dad, and Drew's games."

Strangely enough, Allison was different. She didn't care for sports, but she loved music. She was in the marching band, concert band, and chorus, and always sang in the choir and musicals at church. Mom and Dad never seemed to stress out over her, their youngest. They were as laid back as could be, but yet supportive, and never missed one of her performances. Thus, she adopted this attitude of, "If I do my best, that's good enough." And, already, she was thinking about pursuing music in college in some form—either a major or minor, or at least trying out for band or chorus.

Drew's dad did not drink anymore, but did sometimes brag in front of friends, and in Drew's presence, about his college days. It almost seemed as if he missed the carefree, self-absorbed lifestyle he had lived in college. Drew's mom had never used alcohol, and simply hated any such talk. She wondered why her husband still seemed to miss being an immature kid.

As the end of the spring semester rolled around, Drew was playing baseball and looking forward to the summer before his senior year. But one evening, when he told his parents at supper that he had decided to not play summer ball, there was a fight that was so loud Allison wondered if the neighbors might hear the commotion.

"What do you mean you're not playing baseball this summer, young man!?" Drew's dad's neck was red and he stood up and held his hands on his hips.

"I'm burned out, Dad. I don't enjoy it anymore. It's all I've done since I was five years old. I want to have one summer free—normal like the other kids. Next summer, I'll be in college. Let me just slow down and enjoy my senior year…Please?"

"Well, I doubt if your mom will agree with such a bailing out here just before college scholarship season, Drew! What are you thinking, Son?"

Drew's mom looked scared, and her hands were trembling. "Honey, have you thought this through? What about all the years of sacrifice your father and I have made—to haul you to practice, and on long road trips out of town?...Not to mention the late nights after you've played when your dad had to get up early and go to work the next day."

Drew threw a biscuit across the room. "And that's a good point Mom! How about Dad play this summer for me? It seems all of this has been about him anyway!...When was the last time anyone around here asked ol' Drew if he even wanted to play ball after doing it for twelve years non-stop, day and night?"

"That's enough, Drew," his dad mumbled, almost under his breath. Allison got tears in her eyes as she watched her father slump back in his chair and look listlessly out the window. "And you're right. I can't be you. And you can't be me. I have regretted my entire life not going ahead and playing college ball. I had a scholarship offer you know—from a small school not so far from here. My father would have loved to drive down and watch me play. Mom too. But, I just didn't get it. I wanted to party, and not hit the books, and get by with as little as I could. So, all these years, I've tried to make sure you didn't follow in your dad's footsteps. But, I think I've failed."

Drew had such an opportunity to finally explain to his dad that he was proud of him, and that he had so loved playing ball when he was younger, and that he would maybe play again later on. But instead, he gritted his teeth, "Oh, I am like you Dad. I love to drink. Man, it's so fun. Takes all the pressure away. So, that's what I'll remember about my growing up years. My ol' man bragged about how he used to drink a lot in college. So, one day I tried it, and I liked it too—a lot."

Drew's mom cried out, "Oh no, Drew. Please no."

"Yep Mom. Yes, yes, yes. So, maybe I should have been allowed to go to summer camp after all—even if I missed a game or two. I think my coaches would have survived. Maybe we should have taken normal family trips to the mountains or to the beach like other people do. Maybe at one time, a long time ago, I should have pursued some other hobbies…like fishing, and hiking, and golf, and learning how to fix things like Dad does, and Papaw. I needed that part of my life as a boy growing up. But not anymore. I just need to get away from all of this "stuff" in this family, and go be with my friends."

The good news is, Drew's cry out for help led to a visit with his mom and dad to a counselor, and he admitted he could not drink at all — because it caused him to do crazy things, and he knew he would become a weekend alcoholic, or worse. In fact, the entire family went to the counselor together, and for the first time, began getting healthy. Drew did indeed take some time off from ball, got focused on college and did well, and ended up later on coaching Little League and playing on a church softball team for years. He married, and became a leader in the community.

And on summer Friday nights, Drew's parents again got to watch him play…but in a different way. They had Drew's little boy with them on many of those occasions, and they finally realized that the game really is just a game…to be savored as a wonderful family hobby — not a family obsession.

Questions for Reflection

1. Can you identify your own parenting style and how it may be impacting the growth and achievement of your children?

2. Can you think of situations where a negative self-image caused a child to misbehave and not achieve his or her full potential?

3. What role does emotional intelligence play in effectively disciplining children?

4. Do you know of a situation where a parent forced a child into a life role that did not fit the child's personality and interests?

5. Does your school provide training in 'personality types' for staff and students?

In Stephen Covey's (1990) Principle-Centered Leadership, the essentials of how to live a life focused on timeless, ethical core values are laid out as a very doable plan. For parents, teachers, administrators, coaches, children, students, siblings…living by these principles makes all the difference.

Use Goal Setting and Visualization to Reach the Top
Step 10

"A goal is a dream with a deadline." – Napoleon Hill

This is a simple, yet profound statement. It would be impossible to find any individuals whether young or old who did not have dreams of what they would like to have or achieve in life. However, the real difference between those who fulfill their dreams and those who sputter through life wishing they had better fortunes, is the ability to shape those dreams into definite goals.

Historic Chicago Bears Coach, George Halas, may have put it best when he said, "Many people flounder about in life because they do not have a purpose, an objective toward which to work."

This is such an important component in helping young people achieve success because this is one step that cannot be skipped or rushed through in our life journeys. Without goal setting, all of our great ideas and passion for achieving excellence will never take shape, and we will be left wondering what could have been instead of realizing success.

When thinking about the topic of setting goals, legendary college football coach Lou Holtz is one of the first people who comes to mind. His story is a fantastic example of the power of goal setting. He shares in his autobiography, Wins, Losses, and Lessons, when he was 28 years old, his employment as an assistant coach with the University of South Carolina was terminated. Being left jobless and wondering what his next step should be, his wife gave him the book, The Magic of Thinking Big, by David Schwartz. From this inspiration, Holtz sat down and wrote out 107 goals for his life. These were specific goals, some of which were so lofty that most of us would deem them nearly impossible.

The list included such things as having dinner at the White House, being a guest on The Tonight Show, coaching football at Notre Dame, and winning a national championship. According to an interview by success author Jack Canfield, Holtz had managed by 2008 to accomplish 102 of the 107 goals. Holtz credits writing out his goals as one of the biggest steps in his climb to enormous success. While most people would have wallowed in self-pity, Holtz recorded goals for his life on paper and started his journey to achieving them.

Canfield, who is co-author of the world famous Chicken Soup for the Soul series of books, is also a leading author and speaker in the field of achieving success. In his book, The Success Principles, he outlines steps to help individuals clearly define and achieve goals for their lives. Once specific goals are recorded on paper, one of the major components in this process is then focused on the art of visualization.

Canfield is not the only author to tout the power of visualization. Napoleon Hill, whose quote was provided at the beginning of this chapter, considered this process to be one of the key factors in achieving success with our goals. In his 1937 classic, Think and

Grow Rich, he discusses methods of spending quiet time visualizing our goals as already being accomplished. Much earlier than Hill's work, author Wallace Wattles concentrated on the power of visualization in his 1911 book, The Science of Being Great.

While many people may dismiss this element of achieving goals as nonsense, research is showing the power of what the human mind can help us achieve. For a number of years, medical research has pointed to the mental aspect of healing the human body. However, new findings now point to the power of visualization in other areas of our lives. According to a 2009 article by Angie LeVan, mental practice can sometimes be nearly as effective as physical practice and doing both helps people achieve optimal performance.

LeVan discusses the Olympic success of the Soviet Union back in the 1970's and their use of visualization to prepare for competition. She also points to a popular quote from Jack Nicklaus, who is one of the greatest professional golfers in history. He said, "I never hit a shot, not even in practice, without having a very sharp, in-focus picture of it in my head." Nicklaus combined visualization with actual physical practice to master the game of golf. In addition to these examples, other great athletes, including Michael Jordan and Tiger Woods, have attributed visualization to improving their performance.

It is important to recognize the value of visualization in the goal setting process. Many people believe that the mental aspects of sports are just as important as the physical components. However, this is also true in anything we attempt to accomplish in our lives. By practicing visualization of our goals, we develop a confidence that those goals will become reality, and we also develop the right frame of mind to positively interact with others to impact our success. Also, when we remain focused on our goals through visualization, we recognize opportunities that otherwise might have passed by us in our normal daily lives.

Now that you understand the importance of visualization, let's discuss ways to implement this practice. As it was mentioned at the beginning of this chapter, the first step in setting goals is to record them on paper. Unlike some of the other steps discussed in this book, this step will definitely be easier for an older child or teenager than it would for a younger child.

With a younger child, you may just want to discuss something they would like to accomplish in the short term. It is very difficult for a young child to be able to understand the process of setting a long-term goal or to even really know what they would want that far into the future. It is also good for parents to focus on short-term goals for young children. Otherwise, it would be easy for those long-term goals to actually be goals of the parents for their children rather than the child actually having ownership of the goals.

With teenagers, this process should be able to take shape much easier, and by this point in their lives, it is crucial to begin thinking about both short and long term goals. It would be best for them to record as many of both types of goals as possible, with a total of at least fifty.

This may seem like a large number, but it is vital that young people begin to think out of the box and stretch their minds to think of all the amazing possibilities for their lives. Also, encourage them to be bold and think of anything that they want to accomplish. Remind them of Lou Holtz's far reaching goals that were discussed earlier in this chapter. If they do not record a goal on paper, then more than likely, it will not become a reality.

After this process is complete, the next step is for the young person to go over those goals alone each night before going to bed. It is important not to just read the goals. Instead, they need to take time to read each goal individually and vividly imagine that goal as already accomplished. For instance, if one goal is to graduate from a local university, they should visualize walking across the stage in a graduation gown and earning an actual diploma. Over time, this creates a confidence and belief that this goal will actually become a reality.

In the beginning, if the child is having difficulty completing this process alone, it would be fine for a parent or significant other to sit down and go over each goal and ask the child to visualize the achievement of the goal. However, the child needs to have as much ownership of this process as possible.

It is critical that we encourage young people to complete this process, but at the same time, we need to let them know that many goals, especially long-range goals, may not become a reality for many years. Because of this, we need to make sure they include a mix of short and long-term goals so success can be experienced more quickly in some areas. Also, since young people develop new interests over time, this provides an opportunity to encourage them to add new goals when others are accomplished.

If we help children to develop consistency and diligence in goal setting and visualization, they will begin to experience success that will carry throughout their adult lives.

"Failing to Plan…Thus Planning to Fail!"

Juan's parents just shook their heads and apologized, as their son's principal explained why he had been dropped from the high school academic team.

"He's just not focused. He's doing the same thing he's done with every activity he's tried since coming here his freshman year. It's as if he's bored with success, and once he's proven he can do it, he has no interest in seeing it through to the end."

Juan's parents asked him at dinner to explain his latest 'bail out'. "I don't know. I guess when I was little, everything I tried was easy. Over time, I've developed this thing about having to sacrifice to go the extra mile. I like to try something new, get it done, and move on."

"Juan, that's all well and good," his dad explained while trying to not scold. "But it is a dangerous tendency as your life moves along. Every successful person I know has learned to work hard, over a long period of time…and to set goals, and then map out a plan for realizing those goals. You want to know how long it's taken me to grow my insurance company to where I now have several employees working for me, and can retire in a couple of years if I choose to?"

"But that's different, Dad."

"Is it? Son, you are over halfway through high school. What are your plans for after high school?"

"Oh, I don't know. I guess I'll hang out for a while. You know — take a break."

Juan's mom broke into tears. "Juan, honey, listen to yourself...Do you realize you are one of the brightest kids in your class? And one of the few who has the privileges your father and I can provide for you. Do you not feel some sense of obligation to give back to your school or this town for what you have been blessed with? Or to society? Hasn't life been extra good to you?"

"Yea, Mom–I guess so. But what do you mean — give back?"

Juan's mother could not contain her frustration, and disappointment. "Live a fulfilling, productive life by investing back into the society that has given you every opportunity to live the American Dream...Do you ever discuss this stuff in school?"

"Well, a little — not as much since social studies in seventh grade. These days, for me, it seems school has become more about sports and high test scores."

Juan's dad jumped in. "You mean your school counselor has not met with you yet on what you might be planning to do after you graduate?"

"Well, yea, I guess."

"What did you tell her?"

"I guess I told her I don't know."

Juan's parents suggested that he sit down that evening and begin making a list of goals for his life. And so he could see that life is not all school or work, they asked him to include fun things he wanted to experience or achieve including places he wanted to see or the car he would someday want to own. His parents also asked him to visualize each day those goals coming true for him.

Juan sat down that evening and began making his goal list. As he grew up and continued through high school, college and eventually to a career, he would modify and add to that list many times.

Years later when Juan had his own family and had achieved a successful career and a happy life, he ran across his original goal list and realized how that one evening with his parents changed his life forever!

Questions for Reflection

1. Does your school or school district have an organized process for mentoring students in goal setting and life planning from entry point through senior year?

2. Have you sat down with your children to discuss their own personal goals?

3. Do you know someone who has vast potential, but does not seem to be focused on maximizing that potential? Have you helped offer a lifeline of some kind?

4. Are there adults in your family who have struggled with their career due to not knowing how to set goals and envision achievements?

5. What are three goals you have for your life over the next year? Three years? Five years?

In The Art of the Long View, *by Peter Schwartz (1996), the importance of individual and organizational visioning is stressed, and the art of living into a preferable future through scenarios is offered as a life-changing tool.*

Discovering the Right Career Pathway to Future Success
Step 11

"You have brains in your head. You have feet in your shoes. You can steer yourself any direction you choose. You're on your own, and you know what you know. And you are the only one who'll decide where you'll go." – Dr. Seuss

This profound statement came from all places, a children's book. The Dr. Seuss book *Oh the Places You'll Go!* vividly illustrates the concept that all young people have the unique ability to carve out their own paths to success. Seuss does an outstanding job of instilling confidence in young people to meet life's challenges. Now the big question that remains for parents and educators is how we help the young people in our lives discover that unique path to future career success.

Of all the topics in this book, this is my greatest area of expertise, and one of the reasons for this is my personal experience with pursuing career pathways. As a former principal of a career and technical education (CTE) center, I had the opportunity to design many different career pathways for students to pursue. Due to the success of our career pathways model, I have had the fortune of being invited to speak at education conferences around the nation. When I speak, I call myself "The Poster Child for Career Pathways." When you hear my personal story, you will understand why I use this description.

When I was a teenager, my high school had three diploma types: College Prep, Vocational, and General. I was placed in the College Prep track which I was originally assigned to based on my grades and test scores entering high school. I earned very good grades as a student, and I eventually finished in the top ten of my graduating class.

However, I had never heard of a career pathway when I was in high school. My only experience with selecting a possible college major and career was a meeting with my counselor during my senior year when she presented three options for me to consider. She told me that with my high grade point average and test scores, I should consider a career as a doctor, a lawyer, or possibly an accountant. I remember going home and considering these options. I have always been weak to the sight of blood so I quickly eliminated the medical field as an option. I was actually interested in possibly becoming a lawyer, but when I discovered that law school was three years beyond a bachelor's degree, the thought of seven years of college made me eliminate that possibility.

So, as a process of elimination, I chose to major in accounting at the University of Kentucky even though I had taken no classes in accounting during high school or gained any work experience or shadowing in this career track. What is sad about my situation is that my high school actually had accounting and other business classes, but I was discouraged from taking those courses since they were considered vocational courses. Because I was in a college prep track, I was only encouraged to take additional core classes with no focus on selecting a possible career path.

When I started college, I had to complete general education courses that are required for all majors such as English, math, social sciences, history, science, and art appreciation. Those courses took up the majority of my first two years of college classes. It was not until the second semester of my junior year when I was taking a cost accounting course that the professor made a statement that would change my life forever. She said, "What we are doing today will be very similar to what you will do every day as an accountant." That memory will forever be etched in my mind. I felt as if someone had dropped a ton of bricks on my head. I looked down at the work we were completing in that class, and I knew that I could not spend my life as an accountant!

For the first time in my life, I started to seriously consider possible career pathways and what matched my skill set and passion. As a young child, I had always wanted to be a news broadcaster and later in high school I fell in love with sports and had an interest in being a sports journalist. I wrote sports stories for my high school newspaper. My interest in this area had caused me to pursue a minor in communication. Because I had already taken a few classes in this area, I decided to switch my major to communication and was able to complete my bachelor's degree in four and a half years.

However, I still wasn't completely sure about what career I

wanted to pursue. A stroke of fortune happened to go my way during my last semester of college when the sports editor position came open at my local weekly newspaper in my hometown. I was able to complete my final college courses while writing stories and taking pictures for the newspaper. I continued with that job for two years, but I never quit taking college courses after earning my bachelor's degree. Having the opportunity to work as sports editor allowed me to fulfill a childhood dream, but it also quickly allowed me to see that although there were aspects I really enjoyed with that profession, I knew that it was not going to be a lifelong career for me.

After my graduation from the University of Kentucky, I enrolled at the local community college once again and began exploring different courses of study. One of the first classes I took was an education course, and I soon had the chance to go on a couple of classroom observations. I immediately fell in love with the field of education as I had truly found the place where my passion and talent intersected. I had always loved to help others, and my greatest skill sets were in the areas of written and spoken communication. Because I was only a few credit hours shy of completing my accounting degree, I had completed many different business classes which led me to pursue my teaching certification in business education. Unfortunately for me, it took a total of six and a half years and 200 undergraduate hours to get a degree that I could have obtained in only four years had I only been introduced to this career pathway while I was in high school.

After teaching in the field of business education for six years, I earned my first administrative position as assistant principal and curriculum director at Johnson Central High School, the same school where I had graduated several years earlier. By that point, our school was working with a state and national movement called Tech Prep which emphasized the importance of developing career pathways for high school students. You would have thought that the personal experience I encountered with my own career track would have led me to be an immediate proponent of implementing career pathways. However, as a young school administrator, I was actually resistant to the idea of asking 8th grade students to select a career major before entering high school. I thought it was too early for students to make such a big decision.

Despite my disagreement, our school was responsible for establishing career pathways as part of state grant funding so I worked diligently to refine and implement a complete set of pathways. It was not until about two years later that I began seeing the unexpected benefit of having students select career pathways before entering high school. I soon began seeing several students switch their career majors to a different area after a year or two of high school.

One example of this was our nursing program where often as many as 30 to 40 students per year would sign up with an interest in becoming a nurse. Several years ago, we had a student who went on a clinical experience in a nursing home and observed a nurse drawing blood from a patient for the first time. She nearly passed out and quickly realized that this was not the ideal career for her. Imagine if she had been like me and went on to college and took her general education courses and finally a couple of years later discovered this issue. This experience helped me understand that it is just as important in high school to figure out what you do not want to do with your future as it is to find things you enjoy. These elimination processes are vital to helping students narrow down their possibilities and eventually target the right career pathway.

One of the major cornerstones of following a career pathway is the opportunity to complete work-based learning experiences. The best types of work-based learning include internships, co-ops, or practicums where students get to spend several weeks, a semester or even a school year working in a field related to their chosen career pathway. These experiences are usually volunteer positions, but some participating businesses provide paid opportunities. They are usually two or three hours in length. If these types of work-based learning opportunities are not available for a particular pathway, then shadowing experiences are another option for students. In this type of work-based learning, students follow or shadow an employer in a field related to their chosen career pathway. It is also important for teachers in career major areas to schedule field trips and bring in guest speakers from fields related to various pathways.

As a curriculum director and later a CTE principal, I was able to change our curriculum to the point that we no longer offered college prep and vocational majors. Instead, students would choose a career pathway, and they had an option to pursue an honors diploma which would require more Advanced Placement and honors level coursework but would not affect their career major courses. The beauty of this system is that there are many different exit points for each career pathway, but the career major courses are important for all students, regardless of their test scores and academic achievement level.

I will use the nursing career pathway as an example once again. All students in the program complete clinical experiences at a local nursing home, and they complete the exam to get their CNA (certified nurse aid) certification. Each year, there are high school graduates from the nursing career pathway that will go on to a four-year university to become a registered nurse while other students may choose a two-year degree to become an LPN (licensed practitioner nurse). Finally, some students will complete their CNA certification while in high school and go straight into the workforce at a nursing home or other care facility. Even though the graduates will usually select different exit points, the nursing skills and work experiences they obtain in high school are vital whether they attend a four-year university, a two-year college or enter the workforce directly after graduation.

This career pathway model recognizes the fact that most jobs today require some type of additional training, industry certification or degree beyond a high school diploma. The advantage to starting this process in eighth grade is that students often have the opportunity to earn advanced industry certifications during high school such as certified nurse aide (CNA) in the health science field or A+ certification in the information technology field.

Over the past decade, some important research has been conducted to validate the importance of career pathways and industry certifications. One of the most significant reports was titled, "Pathways to Prosperity: Meeting the Challenge of Preparing Young Americans for the 21st Century." It was released in 2011 by the Harvard Graduate School of Education and was compiled primarily under the leadership of Pathways to Prosperity Project Director William Symonds.

One of the primary findings of this report is that the long standing American goal of all students going to college is failing our economic needs and the futures of our young people. The report outlines the need for a wider system of career pathways with a focus on occupational or industry credentials. In our current system, nearly 70 percent of students enroll in college within two years of graduation. However, only 40 percent of young adults have earned a two-year or four-year degree by the age of 27.

The good news is that only one-third of jobs currently require a bachelor's degree or higher while another 30 percent of jobs require an associate's degree or at least some college. Another important piece of data discussed in the report is that over one quarter of Americans holding only an industry credential are earning more than the average bachelor's degree recipient. There is nothing new about this approach on an international level. Many European countries have fully integrated systems of career pathways, technical education, and apprenticeships during high school to connect young people with work force opportunities aligned to their chosen field of study.

I would strongly encourage parents to explore career pathways options at their child's school. Unfortunately, some smaller schools do not have the staffing capability to offer a wide variety of pathways while many other larger schools still choose to ignore the vital importance of introducing this concept to students before entering high school. If your particular school district does not offer adequate career pathways to students, I would suggest exploring different options for your children.

If you are a teacher leader or school administrator, I think you should explore ways to maximize your staffing capability to offer as many career pathways as possible. There is ongoing research on ways to accomplish this task. Symonds continued his focus on the career pathways movement as he went on to become the director of the Global Pathways Institute at Arizona State University.

As a parent, if you can't find a school to meet the career exploration needs of your children, I would try to organize work-based learning experiences outside of school. If you are going this route, I would suggest that you examine your children's assessment data along with any aptitude tests they may have taken. Usually by high school, you can typically start to see your children's strengths and best subject areas. Finally, it is crucial to have discussions with your child to see where areas of passion exist. For teachers and counselors, this process is also vital to help students make the right decision in selecting a career pathway.

One extremely important factor to remember when helping children select a career pathway is to not force your will on this decision. Even if a child's passion may not be in an area that you had envisioned as a future career choice, it is important to not let your influence be too strong.

A great example of this is a former principal and superintendent that I used to serve under in my school district. He was a great leader and a fantastic parent, but he really wanted his oldest son to go into the medical field. His son, on the other hand, was contemplating a career in education. As a father, he wanted something that he perceived as better for his son, but he had not taken time to examine his son's strongest talent areas. I had taught his son in school, and I could tell that his area of giftedness was his ability to communicate and relate to others. I told my boss that he needed to quit encouraging the medical field because I could tell that his son was not best suited for that career. Thankfully, after taking some college classes, his son switched his major to social studies education, and he has gone on to enjoy an outstanding career as a teacher and later as a school administrator.

Now if a child's passion is in an area where he or she has a very weak skill set, it is equally important to discuss the difficult journey that may lie ahead in pursuing that career pathway. This process refers back to the first step outlined in the book about developing strengths and talents. This is where the success formula (Talent + Passion = Success) can have a big impact. Having an awareness of this principle will give children the ability to determine if their level of passion and work ethic is high enough to compete with others who may have greater talent in their possible career pathways. Sometimes it may take starting in a career pathway to figure out that it is not a great mix of their talents and passion. The great thing about starting the career pathway process early is that it allows more time to change to a different career pathway while still in high school and not in college when it costs time and money. Hopefully, with a great deal of encouragement, the important children in your life will be able to discover where their passion and talent intersect and choose the perfect career pathway for their future success.

"It's Not About the Money"

Alexandria came home from school in tears. Christmas break of her sophomore year in college was here, and she had just received her grades for fall term.

"Mom, I don't want Dad to see these until after the holidays. He will croak!"

"Sis, yes, I'm sure he will sit down and have a talk with you. But, your Dad and I love you very much, and nothing can change that. He will listen, offer advice, and let it go. But, will you listen back?"

"What do you mean, Mom, 'listen back'? I have always been respectful to you and Dad—always."

Alexandria's Mom sat down by her daughter on the couch, as tears welled up in her eyes. "Alex, honey, what were your favorite courses in high school?"

"Literature, music, drama—anything that had to do with the 'arts'. Why mom? What's your point?"

"And when you think back on your childhood, what are your happiest memories?"

"Piano recitals, dance class, writing my own plays, going to 'The Nutcracker' every year about this time with Mamaw and Papaw...What are you getting at, Mom?"

"And this summer, what are you planning to do again?"

"Back at camp, supervising the recreation activities and talent shows each week...MOM, I think I know where you're going with this. Do you realize that there are no jobs that pay a lot of money in these areas I enjoy most?"

"And honey, do you realize that if you aren't fulfilled in your work, it often is such drudgery you will be counting the days to retirement from your first day on the job…Alex, why are your grades so poor—still—here at the end of your sophomore year of college?"

"Because I hate my classes. I hate my major."

"And why did you choose that major?"

"Because all my friends seemed so happy and fulfilled going into careers that pay such good money."

"So you somehow felt like you could pull this off—buy happiness?"

"MOM—it's not like that. I want to have a beautiful home like you and Dad, take my kids on great vacations, travel the world with my future husband…All of that takes lots of money."

"Alex, all of that can come true for anyone who works hard and is passionate about their work—over a period of time."

Alexandria sighed and looked out the window. "Just like Dad used to tell us over and over…'Follow your heart, and you will never have enough time to soak it all in. You will never be out of exciting things to do'."

"Exactly. And what else did he say?"

"Focus on helping people—not acquiring things."

"Alex, sweetie, it's not too late to change your major. It's not too late to look forward to what might be in store just around the bend...What would you really love to do when you complete your college degree?"

"Mom, if I had my ideal life after college--at my fingertips--I'd come back here to this little town, and I'd start a dance studio, and teach private piano lessons. I'd keep working with kids at camp every summer. I'd be an advocate for 'the arts' in the local schools...That would be my dream job."

Alexander's Mom smiled, and cried, and hugged her little girl all at the same time.

"Then do it Honey! Do it!!!"

And Alex did.

Questions for Reflection

1. Has your local school district established career pathways for students to examine and follow during high school?

2. Are there sequences of courses available for students to prepare them for successful transition to the college major or career of their choice?

3. Does your school district have a process for working with students in elementary and especially middle school to begin the career exploration process and discover areas of aptitude and strength?

4. As a parent or significant family member, have you worked with the children in your life to help them discover their areas of talent and passion and begin planning pathways for future success?

William Symonds is a leader in the push for a strong emphasis on career pathways in our schools today. He completed groundbreaking work on the Harvard project, "Pathways to Prosperity: Meeting the Challenge of Preparing Young Americans for the 21st Century." Now as director of the Global Pathways Institute at Arizona State University, Symonds conducts many meetings on the importance of pathways, including the Western Pathways Conference. The Harvard study can be found at: http://agi.harvard.edu/projects/Pathways_to_Prosperity_Feb2011.pdf

Servant Leadership: The Final Step to Enjoying a Life of Success
Step 12

While all of the steps outlined in this book will help young people achieve success in life, there is one key component that is important to help young people enjoy complete fulfillment as an adult. That component is the art of understanding and practicing servant leadership.

While the phrase "servant leadership" sounds like an oxymoron, a deeper look into this topic will explain why this form of leadership is so important to achieving the greatest success in life. Even though the idea of simultaneously serving and leading may seem impossible to many, some of the greatest leadership experts over the past half-century have deemed this approach as crucial to achieving success in today's world. Robert K. Greenleaf, who created the Greenleaf Servant Leadership Center in Indianapolis, Indiana, popularized the term servant leadership in his 1970 essay, "*The Servant as Leader.*" According to Greenleaf, servant leadership is defined as "a philosophy and set of practices that enriches the lives of individuals, builds better organizations and ultimately creates a more just and caring world."

I like to think of servant leadership as an effective way to succeed while creating a win-win situation for everyone involved in an activity. It actually ties in quite well with the principles of motivation that were discussed in Step 2. Servant leadership is strongly related to the ideas of intrinsic motivation, while the opposite of servant leadership is autocratic leadership (which is a top-down model that often evokes motivation by fear). As was mentioned earlier, intrinsic motivation leads to a self-desire to achieve. It also promotes a spirit of teamwork because everyone involved in the organization has a vested interest in the outcomes.

In *The 21 Irrefutable Laws of Leadership*, John Maxwell says, "True leadership cannot be awarded, appointed, or assigned. It comes only from influence, and that can't be mandated. It must be earned. The only thing a title can buy is a little time – either to increase your level of influence with others or to erase it."

Servant leadership, however, goes even deeper than the concept of intrinsic motivation. A servant leader not only empowers the people he or she is in charge of in an organization, this type of leader also works to serve the needs of others. Greenleaf is quoted as saying, "The servant-leader is servant first… It begins with the natural feeling that one wants to serve, to serve first. Then conscious choice brings one to aspire to lead. That person is sharply different from one who is leader first." Helping young people understand this concept at an early age is an important factor in developing an appropriate view of servant leadership.

Autocratic leadership, on the other hand, is based entirely on having a title or position of authority. A lot of people in management aspire to achieve a position of authority in an organization. Once they reach this achievement, they feel like they are not doing their job if they are not controlling all of the employees below them in the organization. One of the only ways a manager can completely control all of his or her employees is to create negative consequences for not completing specified tasks. As we discussed in Step 2, the fear of being reprimanded or losing one's job makes an employee comply with the manager in this leadership model.

Anyone reading this that has ever had a job can relate to this concept. All of us have run into autocratic leaders at some point in time. All of us have had teachers or principals who were autocratic leaders somewhere during our academic journeys. As a matter of fact, if you asked most people who their least favorite teacher was throughout their educational experience, most would point to someone who had autocratic leadership characteristics.

While it is easy for all of us to think of someone who had strong autocratic characteristics, it is much harder for us to look inside ourselves to question our own tendencies. Like most things in life, this is not a completely black and white topic. It is a continuum with complete servant leadership on one side and autocratic leadership on the opposite end.

Many people have tendencies that fall somewhere on that continuum. Often, people may not even show signs of displaying autocratic leadership until they are given a position of authority. Abraham Lincoln said, "Nearly all men can stand adversity, but if you want to test a man's character, give him power." This is such a true statement because many people become enamored with power when given a title or position.

Others just were never taught the principles of servant leadership and feel they must have some autocratic tendencies to be an effective leader. Unfortunately, many people who have a strong drive to earn a management position in an organization often have some autocratic tendencies. This creates a negative cycle and relationship between management and employees.

This is an area where I have had a great deal of experience. As a young teacher taking school administration graduate courses, I had never been introduced to the discipline of leadership. Unfortunately, several of the leaders in my district had autocratic tendencies. As a young aspiring leader, I often wondered if I was harsh enough to be a good leader. Because this trait was modeled as the appropriate form of leadership, I questioned my abilities as a leader. However, as I was introduced to the principles of servant leadership and began to study the work of leaders such as John Maxwell, I quickly began to notice those positive characteristics in a few leaders from my school district.

Then when I was given an opportunity to be assistant high school principal and curriculum director, I had the chance to apply what I had learned. I was worried before taking the position because the previous curriculum director had once expressed to me that if I had that position, most of the teachers would not like me after a couple of years because I would not be able to please them.

When she made the master schedule, she said it was not possible to accommodate the class requests of all the teachers. However, after taking the job, I quickly developed even stronger relationships with the staff at the school. I learned that by practicing servant leadership, we could all become an effective team.

I had noticed that most leaders with autocratic tendencies generally did not empower others and often wanted to withhold knowledge and information to maintain control. As a servant leader, I did the exact opposite. When I worked on the master schedule, I invited other teachers to participate and comment on what they wanted. I always tried diligently to accommodate their requests, but as the previous director had commented, I could not meet all of the requests of the teachers.

The difference for me was that I included teachers in the process. After trying to serve their requests, I would sit down with teachers individually to show why I could or could not complete the requests. I would show alternate options and allow teachers to make suggestions. I learned over time that as long as the teachers knew I had diligently tried to serve all requests, they were pleased with the outcome even when it was not exactly what they wanted.

This was an outstanding early lesson for me in the power of servant leadership. As I have continued to move through my career as a CTE principal, district administrator and high school principal, I have cultivated strong positive relationships with staff members by practicing servant leadership. Most importantly, it is such a wonderful feeling to help others. My career has been extremely gratifying, and I have enjoyed a high level of success, but it has not been the result of individual work on my part.

Instead, I can attribute nearly all of my success to the combined efforts of those I have worked with at each stage of my career. By practicing servant leadership, all of these staff members have equally shared in the design, implementation, and eventual success of each initiative.

Servant leadership can perhaps be best summed up by the words of ancient Chinese philosopher Lao-Tzu, who wrote about these principles in fifth-century BC. He is quoted as saying, "The highest type of ruler is one of whose existence the people are barely aware…. The Sage is self-effacing and scanty of words. When his task is accomplished and things have been completed, all the people say, '*We ourselves have achieved it!*'"

Next Steps for Implementing Servant Leadership

In looking to a future which is limitless with potential, and in empowering and equipping our young people to understand and embrace the core value of 'giving back' to the society that has been so good to them, a key piece is developing servant leaders. For transformational change to take place across our culture, the preferable future must be explored by a younger generation that in unselfish ways chases the call on their lives to make a difference.

What does this transition to a more concentrated stewardship and living into our potential look like? Here are a few clues:

Intentional Leadership Development: Schools, churches, and other civic organizations have a responsibility to model for and mentor the next generation of young leaders. This does not happen very well if there is no well-developed plan. So, moving beyond the status quo formulas that in many ways have not worked very well over the years to new and bold programs that concentrate on the teaching and modeling of unselfish leadership is a crucial piece. If we are not defining and teaching the core values and principles that this society was founded on, and intentionally mentoring/modeling for our young people these principles, then how can we expect them to grow into unselfish adults.

Field Experiences/Internships: The push in education circles to move beyond the school desk and out into the world supports the need to provide young people with real world experiences that expose them to the needs all around them. Most communities have the resources to match students with partners in the workplace, in the non-profit and volunteer arena, on the farms and in the courthouse. How do we expect them to understand the real issues if we are not even exposing them to the opportunities for service all around them?

Scholarships/Sponsorships: Too often, we assume the family and the student are exploring all avenues for financial assistance and acceptance into a post-secondary school of choice that will lead to a meaningful degree and a fulfilling, principled life of service. But in reality, we are still falling short in this key area of preparing students for a future of satisfying contribution back into society. There is an abundance of financial resources and even those who have the ability to underwrite college educations. But, there has to be a plan in place for those who can provide the support to feel the urgency to do so.

Think Tank Work: School, church, government, and civic leaders must come together in agreement on where the gaps lie, and how to move away from toxic habits and into promising practices that point to a future with limitless potential. Kids dropping out of school or turning down opportunities to go on to post-secondary training, chronic alcohol and other drug issues, misuse of entitlement programs, and employment needs that go unresolved are not acceptable and take down entire communities. We must be smarter as a collective group of adult leaders than what we have currently established as the norm.

Vision: What is our collective vision? Are we satisfied with what has evolved as the norm in so many of our communities? What is our preferable future? Then how do we get there? And when do we start, because it's way past time to begin this journey!

Closing Thoughts and Call to Action

It has been such a joy to collaborate on this book. We are excited about what it can mean to parents, young people, and leaders of all ages and in all organizations in perhaps moving beyond the current rhetoric about how bad it is today. Instead, this work can lead us toward real solutions that transform the lives of our next generation of leaders…who will then transform this culture…a culture that has so, so much hanging in the balance.

We want to leave you with one last important thought or actually a call to action. One of the greatest things about this book is that no matter who you are, we all have a role in the lives of young people. We may be parents, aunts, uncles, grandparents, teachers, coaches, employers, or even friends, but all of us make an impact on our youth at some point whether we want to or not. We can choose to lay the responsibility of helping children develop leadership skills off on others, or we can recognize that it takes all of us to make a true difference that will last a lifetime.

A little effort on our part to equip young people with the information and necessary skills to become leaders can reverse the erosion of leadership skills that we have been experiencing for the past several decades. We can no longer foster the attitude that it is someone else's responsibility to help others cultivate leadership skills.

Also, it is important to understand the steps to developing

leadership skills outlined in this book, even though many of these principles challenge our thinking. If we can open our minds and begin to implement these detailed steps, we will see changes in the young people in our lives. If you are a young person reading this book, these steps are not complex and can easily be followed to change your own outcomes. Even as adults, the steps in this book can help us grow as leaders in the process of equipping the young people in our lives to achieve success.

However, this book also has an additional call to action. Hopefully, the government and academic leaders in the world today will begin to see that we must reshape our current educational model to personalize education for all students. We must help students recognize their individual strengths and allow them to explore their areas of passion. We must help each individual student realize where personal talent and passion intersect so success can be achieved. It is our duty to teach the Ladder to Success in a way that students no longer fear failure. Young people must realize at an early age that failure is a tool to achieve success...not the opposite of success!

We must also work to move away from high stakes accountability assessments and more to individual career pathways and plans to help students achieve personal success. We must get away from schools labeling students and expecting all students to work in a cookie cutter curriculum that is tailored to state and national assessments. Actually, leadership should be considered a core subject area. We should have Language Arts, Math, Science, Social Studies and Leadership. It should be considered every bit as important if not more important than other subject areas. Until we start treating it as its own discipline, leadership may never be given the appropriate amount of instructional time in our schools.

Hopefully, this book can serve as a tool to help you make a significant difference in the lives of young people. Writing this book has been an amazing process, and one that has expanded our thinking. We sincerely hope that all young people have the opportunity to follow the steps up **The Ladder to Success**!

– Noel D. Crum and Dr. Rocky Wallace

Notes and Books for Further Reading

Introduction
1. Edison, T.A. (1968). *Diary and sundry observations of Thomas Alva Edison.* Abbey Publishing. (Reprint—New York: Greenwood Press).
2. Maxwell, J.C. (2007). *Talent is never enough.* Nashville: Thomas Nelson.

Step 1: Developing Strengths and Talents
1. Buckingham, M., and D.O. Clifton. (2001). *Now, discover your strengths.* New York, NY: The Free Press.

Step 2: Motivation Understood
1. Pink, D. (2009). *Drive.* New York, NY: Riverhead Books.

Step 3: Failing Up the Ladder to Success
1. Youssef, I. (2011). *The great secret of life.* Bloomington, IN: Xlibris Corporation.

Step 4: Responsibility Develops Self-Discipline and Self-Confidence
1. Citrin, J.M., and R.A. Smith. (2003). *The 5 patterns of extraordinary careers.* New York, NY: Crown Business.

Step 5: Attitude Will Determine Your Altitude

1. Maxwell, J.C. (2006). *The difference maker*. Nashville: Thomas Nelson.
2. Vujicic, N. (2012). *Life without limits: Inspiration for a ridiculously good life*. Colorado Springs: Waterbrook Press.
3. Johnson, E.M., and W. Novak. (1992). *My life*. New York: Random House.
4. Sandborn, M. (2002). *The fred factor*. Colorado Springs: Waterbrook Press.

Step 6: Cultivating Positive Communication Skills

1. Ryan, F., Jr. (1995). *The great communicator*. New York: Perennial.
2. Clinton, W. J. (2004). *My life*. New York: Alfred Aknoph, Publisher.
3. http://uspolitics.about.com/od/presidenc1/tp/End-of-Term-Presidential-Approval-Ratings.htm
4. Toland, J. (1976). *Adolph Hitler: The definitive biography*. New York: Anchor Books.
5. Ortberg, J. (2010). *The ME I want to be*. Grand Rapids, MI: Zondervan.
6. Maxwell, J.C. (2010). *Everyone communicates few connect*. Nashville: Thomas Nelson.

Step 7: Foster a Competitive Spirit

1. Lombardi, V., Jr. (2003). *The essential Vince Lombardi*. New York: McGraw Hill.
2. Gladwell, M. (2008). *Outliers*. New York, NY: Little, Brown and Company.

Step 8: Two P's in a Pod – Perseverance and Perfection

1. Greenspon, T. (2001). *Freeing Our Families from Perfectionism*. Minneapolis: Free Spirit.
2. Hamachek, D. E. (1978). Psychodynamics of normal and neurotic perfectionism. *Psychology*, 15, 27-33.
3. The Arbinger Institute. (2000). *Leadership and self-deception*. San Francisco, CA: Berrett-Koehler Publishers, Inc.

Step 9: Unlocking the Potential in a Difficult Child

1. http://parenting.com/article/preventing-tween-behavior-problems.
2. Covey, S.R. (1991). *Principle-centered leadership*. New York, NY: Summit Books.

Step 10: Use Goal Setting and Visualization to Reach the Top

1. Hill, N. (1937). *Think and grow rich*. New York: The Penguin Group.
2. Davis, J. (2005). *Papa bear: The life and legacy of George Halas*. New York: McGraw-Hill.
3. Holtz, L. (2007). *Wins, losses, and lessons: An autobiography*. New York: HarperCollins.
4. Canfield, J. (2005). *The success principles*. New York: HarperCollins.
5. Waddles, W. (1911). *The science of being great*. New York: Firework Press. Colorado Springs: Waterbrook Press.
6. http://psychologytoday.com/blog/flourish/200912/seeing-is-believing-the-power-visualization.
7. Schwartz, P. (1991). *The art of the long view*. New York, NY: Doubleday.

Step 11: Discovering the Right Career Pathway to Future Success

1. Suess, D. (1990). Oh the Places You'll Go! New York: Random House.
2. http://agi.harvard.edu/projects/Pathways_to_Prosperity_Feb2011.pdf

Step 12: Servant Leadership: The Final Step to ENJOYING a Life of Success

1. Greenleaf, R.K. (1970). The servant as leader. Indianapolis: Greenleaf Center for Servant Leadership.
2. Maxwell, J.C. (1998). *The 21 irrefutable laws of leadership.* Nashville: Thomas Nelson.
3. http://quotationspage.com/subjects/character.
4. http://banyanstrategics.com/about-us-3/servant-leadership/

About the Authors

Noel Crum is currently the Principal at Johnson Central High School. He has over twenty years of experience in the field of education as he has served in the capacity of teacher, curriculum director, CTE principal, high school principal and district level administrator. He designed new career pathways which led to the creation of the Johnson Central Career and Technical Center where he served as the first principal. He has given numerous presentations across the United States on career pathways and youth leadership. He and his wife Stacy have three children (Reiley, Ally, and Sawyer) and live just outside of Paintsville, Kentucky.

Dr. Rocky Wallace is Associate Professor, Graduate Education, and is the Coordinator of the Principal Licensure Program at Asbury University. He is a former principal of a Kentucky and U.S. Blue Ribbon School, and has authored four previous books on the topics of principalship and servant leadership. He has also co-authored three other books on the connection between healthy relationships in the classroom and school culture. He and his wife Denise have two daughters, Lauren (husband Ely), and Bethany (husband Troy), and live on 16 acres in the country near Paris, Kentucky.

For more information about The Ladder to Success, including how to order more copies of the book or to contact the authors about speaking engagements, please visit the following website:

www.laddertosuccess.org

www.ingramcontent.com/pod-product-compliance
Lightning Source LLC
LaVergne TN
LVHW051051080426
835508LV00019B/1811